INDUSTRIAL MARKETING RESEARCH

TECHNIQUES & PRACTICES

Donald D. Lee
Professor of Management
Widener College
Chester, PA 19013

INDUSTRIAL MARKETING RESEARCH

Donald D. Lee

a **TECHNOMIC**® publication
TECHNOMIC Publishing Co., Inc.
265 Post Road West, Westport, CT. 06880

ISBN 0-87762-248-5
Library of Congress Card No. 77-95307
Printed in U. S. A.

TABLE OF CONTENTS

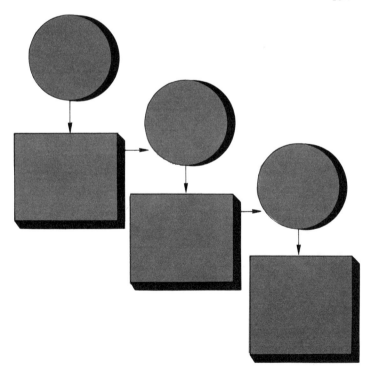

PREFACE

Marketing research is needed in every business enterprise, and it is performed in every successful firm. The function may not be so named; in fact, in some cases it may not even be recognized as marketing research. It may be formalized as a separate unit of several persons, or it may be performed along with other duties by a single individual. It may be organized and chartered to serve a whole corporation, or only a single division.

"Marketing research as a function can be, and is, carried out in many different departments, such as Commercial Development, Planning, Corporate Development, Market Development, R & D, etc... The name of the department may change, but the function continues."*

Although marketing research for *consumer goods* is well known, widely taught and expounded in numerous texts and reference books, both in the United States and abroad, marketing research for *industrial goods* is almost totally ignored in courses and books. Few except the practitioners of industrial marketing research know how much it differs from consumer marketing research.

In the 200,000 or more U.S. firms manufacturing industrial goods, there must be more than 200,000 persons practicing marketing research, at least part-time. Large firms have 50 or more full-time marketing researchers. Many firms, small and large, also employ marketing research consultants.

It is therefore anachronistic that the modern art and science of industrial marketing research is taught largely by the apprenticeship method of the Middle Ages. The typical industrial marketing researcher is an engineer or scientist who, after perhaps several years in production, research and/or marketing, was assigned to the marketing research function with no formal training in the subject. Having no published textbook available, he learned his new responsibilities and methods by being apprenticed to an experienced marketing researcher, possibly with the aid of a short course of the type offered by the Chemical Marketing Research Association and the very few other professional societies interested in the subject.

This book was written for

- college students of marketing
- new practitioners in industry
- experienced practitioners, who may want to learn new techniques
- corporate users of marketing research, who may want to learn what the function can do for them.

It is a "how to" type of book, designed to be pragmatic rather than theoretical, and is written in language I hope will be acceptable to all four audiences. It has been used by MBA candidates at Widener College, some of whom have been kind enough to offer suggestions for greater clarity and utility.

I am deeply indebted to Russell C. Kidder of Stauffer Chemical Co , William E.

---

*Private communication, Aug. 30, 1976, from Russell C. Kidder, Past President of the Chemical Marketing Research Association, and Manager of Commercial Development, Specialty Chemical Division, Stauffer Chemical Company, Westport, Connecticut.

i

Pearson of Dow Chemical U.S.A., and Robert S. Thomas of B.F. Goodrich Chemical Company, who patiently read and commented on my first draft. I am even more obligated to Carl S. Carlson of Shaheen Natural Resources Co., R. M. "Pete ' Hull of Hull and Company, William E. Marklewitz of Dow Chemical Co., and (again) to Russell C. Kidder of Stauffer Chemical Co., who not only read my third and fifth drafts very thoroughly, but also met with me on three occasions, as an ad hoc Book Review Committee of the Chemical Marketing Research Association, to give me their suggestions, chapter by chapter and line by line. The book reflects, faithfully, I hope, the improvements they offered. Where it fails in any way, the fault is mine alone.

Special thanks and tribute go to Mrs. Germaine V. Curliss, who deciphered my hieroglyphics, typed all of the several drafts and partial revisions, and who did a superb job of proofreading.

CHAPTER 1

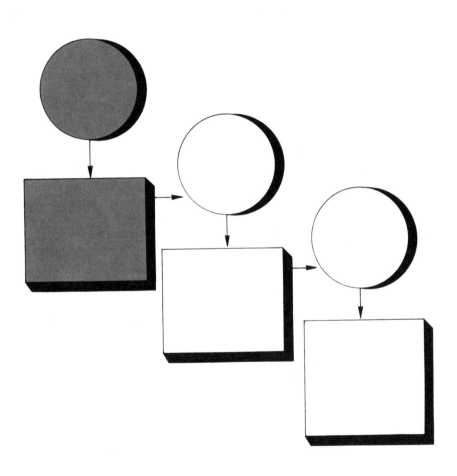

THE GOALS OF INDUSTRIAL MARKETING RESEARCH

A. Characteristics of Industrial Marketing

To most people, the marketing of industrial goods seems simple and almost automatic. They suppose the user simply places his orders with suppliers that make and deliver. They tend to assume that types and qualities are standardized and that an adequate quantity is always available. Hence, they think that very little marketing effort is required.

If they learned from economists that the user's demand is a "derived demand", they probably also visualize it as being quite steady or at least easily predictable.

The truth is quite the opposite.

Industrial marketing of most materials, components, supplies, equipment and services is extremely competitive. Users search continually for ways to cut costs of purchases, and alert suppliers try to satisfy this need by devising less-costly replacements for traditional goods.

Demand for industrial goods is more variable than for consumer goods because of the multiplier effect of inventories that are built up when sales rise and depleted when sales drop. The effect on suppliers is to cause periods of feast and famine, not only in terms of demand but also (and even more painfully) in terms of price.

By definition, industrial goods are materials, components, supplies and equipment used to make other goods, industrial and/or consumer. The conversion process may be chemical, mechanical or both, and the product may be sold to the ultimate consumer or to another processor for further conversion (see Figure 1−1). Requirements for the industrial goods involved in the first transaction are "derived demands". To understand the market fully and to measure and forecast demand intelligently requires knowledge of the markets for the conversion products. Therefore, the marketer of industrial goods must know the characteristics and needs of not only his direct customer, the *processor*, but also his customer's customer, the *end-user*.

Figure 1−1 is a generalized case. Exceptions abound, including the simpler case of sale directly to an end-user (e.g., lumber for furniture) and more complicated cases in which several processors participate in sequence (e.g., petroleum to petro-chemicals to plastics to components for appliances).

A manager needs much information about his markets, both the processors to whom he sells directly, and the end-users who are indirect customers. He needs to know consumer demands for the end-products, what his customers are buying and at what price, what his competitors are selling and on what terms, and the technical, economic, legal, political and sociological trends that may influence his business. He needs perceptive analysis, integration and interpretation of that information, and he needs creative, judicious recommendations to establish, strengthen or change his marketing strategy.

As a product progresses through its life cycle from concept to maturity and perhaps obsolescence, a multitude of decisions must be made, altered, abandoned and/or re-made relating to all the elements of marketing strategy:
- product attributes and differentiation
- price structure and terms

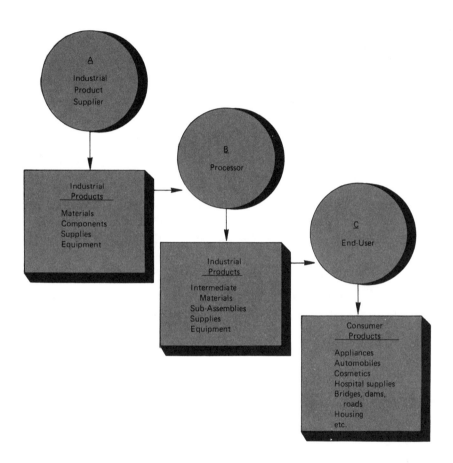

Figure 1-1 Supplier/Processor/End-User Relationships

○ advertising, promotion and sales aids
○ personal selling
○ distribution channels
○ marketing organization
○ marketing budget
○ contingency plans.[1]

Intelligent decisions must be based on the most reliable information available. In the average company, new plant investment and manufacturing cost is estimated to within ±10% of actual. However, future sales volume estimates may prove to be in error by 20—30%; and estimates of future prices too frequently miss by as much as ±50%. The errors in estimating earnings and return on investment are further exaggerated because a 1% error in sales price or volume may mean a 3—10% error in profit.

Managers never have all of the facts for making decisions. They must deal with unpredictable influences and complex relationships, such as customer confidence, customer preferences, competitors' activities, government regulations, international tensions and economic trends. Furthermore, marketing decisions will seldom wait for exhaustive searches. So the goal of marketing research is not perfect information, but an *optimum combination of useful information within acceptable time and cost limits*. The aim of the manager is to make fewer guesses and take smaller risks.

B. What is Marketing Research?

Numerous attempts have been made to define the functions and responsibilities of marketing research in a few words, but none of the definitions satisfies everyone.[2] One reason is that consumer and industrial marketing research differ so extensively in method. Furthermore, the scope of marketing research varies from one firm to another.

In very broad terms, effective marketing research comprises a constant probing of the market environment to scrutinize and reappraise existing markets, to find new markets, to define the specifications of ideal products for those markets, to measure and forecast the demands of the markets, to forecast prices, and to devise and recommend new and/or better marketing strategies to deliver the products to the markets at acceptable profit levels. It includes frequent reviews of the firm's existing product line to ascertain which items, if any, should be withdrawn or differentiated to satisfy specific market segments. It may also explore ways of improving the firm's marketing and financial position through re-selling, licensing, acqusition and merger.

These activities apply to marketing research for both consumer goods and industrial goods, but many of the methods and descriptive terms differ. For example,

---

[1] Hansen, *Marketing: Text, and Cases,* Irwin, 4th ed. 1977, pp. 765—785. McCarthy, *Basic Marketing,* Irwin, 5th ed., 1975, pp. 74—81.

[2] The American Marketing Association described marketing research as "The systematic gathering, recording and analyzing of data about problems relating to the marketing of goods and services".

consumer goods marketing researchers speak of markets segmented by demographic characteristics (age, sex, income, life style, etc.) of the consuming public. They think of products distinguished by taste, color, design, styling, ego-appeal, status symbolism, and conformity with the fad of the moment. Surveys to measure consumer preference and consumption must deal with largely subjective data. Usually, these data are gathered from representative samples of the public and must be interpreted with the aid of statistics.[3]

Industrial goods marketing researchers, on the other hand, generally deal with scientifically-measurable product properties such as density and tensile strength of materials, horsepower rating of motors, efficiency of generators, thermal conductivity of insulating board and covering power of pigments. They frequently gather quantitative demand data from all or most of the relatively few industrial firms that constitute a market.[4]

Both categories of marketing researchers supply factual information, opinions, interpretations and recommendations needed by various management functions to understand the marketing environment and make intelligent decisions.

The functions and responsibilities of marketing research can be classified and defined more specifically in eight major categories.

○ *Identifying and Characterizing Markets*

A market usually comprises one or more industries and/or segments of industries and can be identified comprehensively by describing those industries and/or segments, in terms of their activities, products, technologies, sizes and trends (as discussed in more detail in Chapter 4).

Specific customers and end-users in a market sometimes deserve a more detailed description or "profile" (see Chapter 4) because of their size and importance as consumers and leaders in the market.

Major competitors, also, should be profiled for a thorough understanding and appreciation of a market and the anticipated business environment.

Market identification studies vary tremendously in scope and depth. The simplest identification is a prospect list for the firm's sales representatives: the most complex might include a recommendation for acquisition of a customer to achieve forward integration.

○ *Defining Products to Satisfy Markets*

While it is obvious that a marketing researcher must have a product or product concept in mind before he or she can identify its market, it does not always follow that the actual or visualized product truly meets the needs of the market. The present and/or future uses of the product must be known or imagined and the desired specifications (properties and performance) must be ascertained as precisely as possible. This permits estimating the "value-in-use" of the product and its "opportunity" (demand at saturation), as are described in Chapter 8.

---

[3] Buzzell, Cox & Brown, *Marketing Research and Information Systems,* McGraw-Hill, 1969, pp. 113–199.
[4] Dodge, *Industrial Marketing,* McGraw-Hill, 1970, pp. 111–143.
Giragosian, *Chemical Marketing Research,* Reinhold, 1967, pp. 32–39.
Williams, *Technical Market Research,* Roger Williams Technical & Economic Services Inc., 1962.

With such information, a marketing researcher can find new markets or segments attainable by product improvement and differentiation.

○ *Measuring Current Demand*

Having carefully defined a product and identified its present markets, a marketing researcher could assemble statistics to measure current demand, using one or more of the techniques described in Chapter 5. Published data ("secondary sources") might be adequate in some cases, but it would often be necessary to collect and analyze original data from processors and/or end-users ("primary sources") using questionnaires and interviews (see Chapter 3 for methods).

○ *Forecasting Future Demand*

In our dynamic economy, both total industry demand and individual firms' sales vary with time. New products grow, old products are replaced and every supplier's market share is subject to change. Techniques for demand forecasting are described in Chapter 6.

○ *Forecasting Price*

No major marketing research study is complete without a price forecast, as well as a demand forecast. Both short-range and long-range methods are described in Chapter 7.

○ *Marketing Strategy Recommendations*

Although policies vary in this regard, most firms expect their marketing researchers to conclude major studies with recommendations for action.

The new, or improved, strategy may emerge logically from the facts and opinions uncovered in a market study, without any major calculations, or it may be derived only after some sort of mathematical (perhaps computerized) model has been constructed and used for simulations to explore the possible effects on market share, sales and profits of various alternative strategies (see Chapter 9).

Depending on the anticipated influences of developing technology, competitive threats, new legislation and so on, a marketing research study may recommend plant expansion, product differentiation, merger or withdrawal of a dying product from the market.

○ *Special Services*

It is unusual, but neither illogical nor unknown, for a marketing researcher to assist management in reaching creative decisions with decision trees, critical path diagrams, concept and market testing programs and end-use development (see Chapter 10).

○ *Monitoring and Follow-Up*

Properly applied, marketing research is based on a thorough knowledge of products and markets, including the historical record of sales volume, market share and price trends. It is not implied that the marketing researcher should be a super-clerk, collecting and keeping books full of statistics, for computerized marketing information systems do this much more effectively (see Chapter 9), but rather that regular, periodic attention should be given to the records.

Monitoring is especially important just before and during the implementation of any new marketing program based on recommendations of a recent marketing research study. An effective marketing researcher wants his or her reports to be read, understood and used, and is eager to observe (1) how the reaction in the market place compares with that visualized in the study, and (2) what contribution the study makes to company operations.

C. The Position of Marketing Research in the Company Organization

Marketing Research is a staff group, removed from the day-to-day problems of running the business, and given the opportunity to think creatively. Historically, the function being a responsibility of the Sales or Marketing Division, the individual or the group assigned was a part of that division in most firms.

The advantages of this positioning are derivatives of this proximity; the easy access to sales records, to customer call reports, to the observations of the field sales force, to the opinions and expertise of district managers, etc., and through these contacts, the easy access to customer reactions (acceptance, complaint, need). An occasional transfer of personnel from Marketing Research to Field Sales (or to some other section of the Marketing Division), and vice versa, insures cross-fertilization and good rapport.

The danger inherent in this positioning is that a strong-willed Marketing Director may exert too much influence and the research may become less than objective.

It is imperative that the Marketing Research Section have ready access to marketing people and their know-how, and that it earn and enjoy the backing of top marketing management; and it is apparent that this backing is most likely to be given if the Marketing Research Section is a part of the Marketing Department, reporting to the top marketing executive.[5]

Nevertheless, Marketing Research is organizationally separated from Marketing in many firms. Sometimes this is done so that it can serve the entire corporation more effectively, sometimes so that it can be combined with Planning or some other section, sometimes to insure the objectivity mentioned above, and sometimes merely because influential members of Management want it elsewhere (perhaps even to minimize a personality conflict).

In a few very large firms, the several divisional marketing research sections are supplemented by a corporate group that

- ○ undertakes studies of markets and products not yet yet assigned to a division
- ○ undertakes studies covering the interests of several divisions
- ○ can apply highly sophisticated techniques to a study being made by a divisional section
- ○ offers training courses for personnel newly assigned to divisional sections
- ○ serves as a talent pool for peak load (temporary) assignment to a division.

---

[5] *Marketing, Business and Commercial Research in Industry,* The Conference Board, 1964, pp. 7–9.

D. Interfaces With Other Departments

Although Marketing Research was originally created to serve Marketing, it should and does make valuable contributions to General Management, to Business Research, to Corporate Planning, to Research and Development (R & D) or Engineering Design and Development (ED & D), to Distribution, and occasionally to Manufacturing and to Purchasing. The relative impact of its contributions to these departments will vary from firm to firm, and may be greatest in market-oriented companies selling innovative products to rapidly growing markets.

The flows should be two-way in all cases (see Figure 1−2), for

o *General Management* sets the stage for marketing research by providing policy and over-all long-range objectives of the firm; and it receives from Marketing Research forecasts of demand and price, and recommendations for strategy

o *Business Research or Corporate Planning* supplies more detailed goals and receives forecasts, warnings of expansion needs, and identification of acquisition prospects

o *Marketing* provides marketing intelligence of all kinds, including indications of product and service needs of customers, and the activities of competitors; and it receives the full range of marketing research results − strategy recommendations, marketing intelligence, forecasts, opportunity estimates, prospect lists, product ideas, concept and market testing, end-use development, decision trees and critical path diagrams

o *R&D or ED & D* supplies potential new product concepts and receives estimates of the markets for those potential products, plus early warnings of customer needs for still other new or improved products

o *Distribution* provides indications of needs for more effective channels and/or warehousing, and receives names of prospective new distributors and suggestions for optimum warehouse locations

o *Manufacturing and Purchasing* warn of raw materials shortages or delivery bottlenecks, and receive make-or-buy studies and suggestions of alternative sources.

It naturally follows that the emphasis by Marketing Research on one or more of the above contributions will be influenced by its position in the organization. A marketing researcher reporting to General Management or to Corporate Planning is more aware of over-all corporate needs. Consequently, he or she is influenced to think more broadly and to direct more effort to the total firm.

Similarly, a marketing researcher situated in R&D, in Engineering Design, in Commercial Development or in Market Development probably tends to be more interested in new products, new markets and product differentiation than in existing products.

E. The Trend Toward Business Research

There has always been some tendency for marketing researchers to exhibit an interest in manufacturing and finance, because a recommendation that a new product be launched or that sales be extended into an additional market can be implemented only provided production facilities and capital are available. Marketing researchers have frequently made cost estimates and return on investment

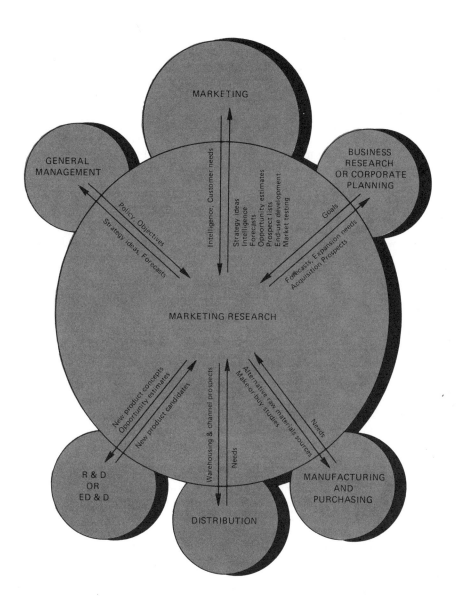

MARKETING

GENERAL
MANAGEMENT

BUSINESS
RESEARCH
OR CORPORATE
PLANNING

Intelligence; Customer needs

Strategy ideas
Intelligence
Forecasts
Opportunity estimates
Prospect lists
End-use development
Market testing

Goals

Policy, Objectives

Strategy ideas, Forecasts

Forecasts, Expansion needs
Acquisition Prospects

MARKETING RESEARCH

New product concepts
Opportunity estimates

New product candidates

Warehousing & channel prospects

Needs

Alternative raw materials sources
Make-or-buy studies

Needs

R & D
OR
ED & D

DISTRIBUTION

MANUFACTURING
AND
PURCHASING

Figure 1-2 Marketing Research Interfaces

calculations, and included these in their reports, to show the benefits of their strategic suggestions.

Furthermore, because marketing research utilizes techniques for finding facts, making estimates, analyzing, evaluating, drawing conclusions and making recommendations with the objective of persuading management to act, its practitioners are equipped with many of the skills required for what is commonly called corporate planning.

Especially with the current emphasis on market orientation, the executives of many firms are seriously interested in ideas that originate in their marketing departments. Therefore, those marketing researchers who fulfill their mission as the "eyes and ears" of industry are receiving favorable attention from top management.

More or less simultaneously with the emphasis on market orientation, there is occurring a trend (less apparent and less frequently discussed in business literature) away from the special project type of corporate planning, and toward continuous surveillance of the firm's performance by staff individuals and groups. The function is not new. It has been a major responsibility of presidents, directors and other top officials, and it still is; but the assignment of the function, on a continuous basis, to highly qualified staff was rare until recently.

Reference to one of the earliest forms of this practice was made by Drucker,[6] who related the creation by the Deutsche Bank in 1870 of a small group of high-potential, young men to keep all branch managers apprised of decisions and successful innovations in that geographically scattered organization. Drucker extrapolated from that example to suggest a business research group staffed with young persons who had demonstrated management potential. It was his suggestion that they be given the assignment for perhaps five to eight years, then be promoted into higher management positions (assuming they had performed well).

Such a business research group might still embark on major studies, but its day-to-day responsibility would be for a running audit of performance against goals, motivation of managers and the research for expansion opportunities, including acquisitions and mergers. Effective conduct of this work requires thorough and extensive observation and evaluation, including contributions from research, engieering, manufacturing, finance, personnel and sometimes legal departments, as well as from marketing. It is fulltime venture analysis in its complete sense.[7]

To be effective, the business researchers must know the company, its products, its people, its strengths and its weaknesses, *intimately*. They must have the respect and confidence of middle and lower management on whom they must depend for many of their facts, opinions and interpretations. And they must have the active, on-going support of top management so that their observations and recommendations will not be ignored.

Business researchers must be experienced, informed, circumspect, articulate and highly judicious. It therefore seems logical when an experienced, capable marketing researcher is transferred to a business research position.

---

[6] Drucker, "New/Old Top Management Aids: The Executive Secretariat", *Harvard Business Review*, Sept.–Oct., 1975, pp. 6–8.

[7] Uyterhoeven, Ackerman & Rosenblum, *Strategy and Organization: Text and Cases in General Management*, Irwin, 1973.

QUESTIONS

1. Compare and contrast the functions of marketing research vis-a-vis scientific research (R & D) and engineering design.

2. In what ways does marketing research compete with scientific research and engineering design? In what ways can they be complementary?

3. Ultimately, almost every industrial product is used in the manufacture of something for the consumer. Why should industrial marketing researchers not be more concerned with consumer opinion?

4. Figure 1–2 shows marketing research utilizing information from almost every division of a firm, and serving each in some way. Does this mean the marketing research organization would be most effective if it reported directly to top management? Why, or why not?

CHAPTER 2

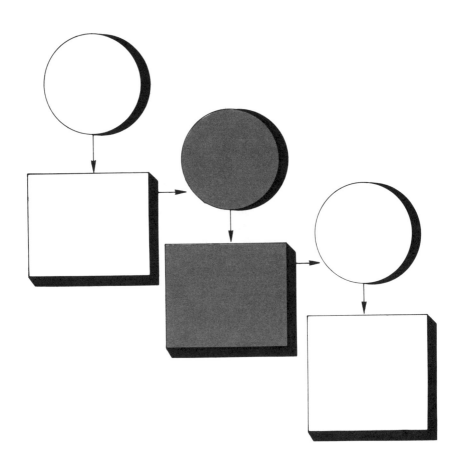

ADMINISTRATION AND PERSONNEL

A. Initiating Marketing Research Assignments

It was seen in the preceding chapter that some marketing research studies are largely descriptive, others are highly analytical and quantitative, and that almost all lead to some assessment of the future. Before discussing these in detail, it is appropriate to consider how these tasks are initiated, by whom they are conducted and some of the administrative tasks of a marketing research organization.

Most marketing research assignments probably are initiated by the division managers of the firm; i.e., by the "clients" of the Marketing Research Section. They need market information, forecasts and strategy recommendations in order to launch new ventures, to strengthen marketing programs, to meet competitive threats, etc. Simultaneously, alert marketing researchers will be watching market developments and generating ideas, and they should be encouraged to suggest studies they might make to help their clients. In some firms, Marketing Research is authorized to undertake self-generated projects without prior approval.

Some marketing research studies are relatively compact, self-contained "projects", requiring intensive study over a relatively short period of time. Others will take a low-level (i.e., part-time) effort extended over a long period of time. Examples of the first type are market identification and company profile studies, the construction of a marketing model and the derivation of an econometric forecast. In the second category fall continuing marketing intelligence, the testing of a forecasting equation for its forecasting reliability, the monitoring and revision of a marketing information system, and the updating of a marketing model as new competitive products and new uses materialize.

B. Budgeting

Much has been written on budgeting, recording and controlling expenditures of staff groups, and on the allocation of charges as overhead to the client(s) served. Every firm has its own system.

Just two points deserve attention here.

(1) It is a salutary exercise for the Marketing Research Manager to prepare an annual budget, with justifications for the money, personnel and auxiliary expenditures he wants. It may also be an occasion for him to review formally with his clients what his marketing researchers have done for them in the current year, and could do in the coming year. It certainly is an appropriate time to ask for inclusion in the budget of a major allocation such as would be required to cover design of a model, revision of a marketing information system, etc.

(2) If Marketing Research is to do most for a client, it should be on *his* job continuously. That is to say, it should be watching his sales, observing his markets, monitoring his competitors, and thinking about his problems *all* the time (see Chapter 1, Section B, What is Marketing Research?). This militates against a project system of assigning work and of budgeting, and lends support to the continuing type of assignment, *including* any special projects. The

project system is customary, however, when a client can not afford full-time assignment, and when a completely new venture is being examined.

C. Recruiting and Training Marketing Researchers

For a position of such central and vital importance, one must look for men and women having good judgment, intellectual curiosity, broad perspective and high intelligence.

There are substantially no new graduates trained in industrial marketing research, for the subject is ignored at most schools at the present time. Former sales and technical service men and women with an interest (and some ability) in mathematics, statistics and/or management science probably will be best qualified among those recruited from within the firm.

New graduates with training in some combination of science or engineering and business, also may develop into very satisfactory marketing researchers, if they are motivated toward a career in marketing. Experience has shown that a technical undergraduate degree, plus an MBA, plus a desire to sell can produce a person who quickly learns the techniques and the business. Naturally, the Manager must keep some experienced marketing researchers available to train and advise the new recruits.

Probably the best way to indoctrinate a new marketing researcher is to apprentice him or her to an "old pro"; that is, to an experienced member of the Section. The apprentice should, or course, be introduced to the Section's files of completed reports, its library of pertinent publications and statistics, the Marketing Information System; and he or she should be encouraged to read regularly a business newspaper and the trade journals that cover the firm's fields of interest. If it can be arranged, he or she should attend program discussions, product review meetings and district sales meetings relating to the product line of his or her assignment. Given an opportunity to participate by reporting the results of a recent study, the marketing researcher can promote the Section and his or her image as an ally and aide.

There probably will always be some controversy among marketing research people over the advantages and disadvantages of staffing with

○ career marketing research specialists, versus

○ young, high-potential candidates for management positions.

It would seem that each system has been successful in certain companies and that the choice should depend largely on the personnel policy of the company, coupled with the desires of the employee.

The advantages of career researchers are that they have the opportunity to become experts in sophisticated techniques, such as designing and using models; and they can learn the firm's products, markets and organization so well as to become recognized and trusted sources of marketing information and strategies.

The disadvantages are that few people really are content to continue in the same function indefinitely, and that they may become so enamored of techniques and jargon as to be avoided and ignored by pragmatic marketing personnel who may come to regard them as "ivory tower" types.

The advantages of having young, high-potential management candidates are that they usually have a broad outlook, an interest in learning all they can about the firm, and mature judgment. Especially if they aspire to marketing management assignments, they will exhibit an intense desire to know marketing people, products, programs and problems. This in turn, should bring them to the attention of marketing managers who will see them as potential Sales Technologists, Sales Representatives, Product Specialists, etc.

The disadvantages are that such persons may be too restless to take the time to learn the more sophisticated techniques, or to do the routine tasks thoroughly. Their results may not be trusted. One or more of the "old pro" researchers must be available to guide them.

D. Qualifications of the Marketing Research Manager

Aside from possessing business acumen, good judgment and managing ability, the Manager *must know marketing*. He or she must have the respect and confidence of marketing management people, and needs to be acquainted with a large proportion of the company's customers. Experience as a sales representative or product manager provides an excellent background.

In addition, the Manager should be able to
○ communicate effectively with management science and computer personnel
○ sell the services of the Section
○ teach and lead subordinates
○ facilitate the relationships between the marketing researchers and their clients.

E. Outside Consultants

The classical "make or buy" decision applies to marketing research as well as to raw materials. If an outside consultant can provide instant expertise needed in designing a model or refining an information system, he may save not only money, but also precious time. A consultant may have widespread and influential contacts from whom he could obtain important information about markets, products, needs, trends, and so on.

Multi-client studies made by consultants usually are very thorough and well-documented. Because costs are spread among several clients, the price to any one client is almost invariably far less than the cost of a comparable study by one client's own personnel. The major drawback is the availability of the study results to others.

A major advantage offered by consultants is the objectivity with which they can collect, analyze and interpret facts about markets and marketing. They are sometimes employed to provide an independent source when two factions within a firm are uncompromising.

There also are types of studies requiring information unavailable to a supplier. Customers, and particularly competitors, will not answer certain questions if they are asked by a supplier, and they may bias their answers to other questions. Here, a consultant can be neutral, can assure confidentiality of source, and may promise that only aggregated figures will be passed on to his client, thus protecting his respondents.

Finally, a company that is contemplating entry into a market may need the services of a consultant to explore its opportunity without revealing its identity to established suppliers.

The consultant should be given as much background information as he needs, within the limits of reasonable security. The Marketing Research Manager should participate in his selection, see that he is adequately briefed, maintain contact as the study proceeds, and know the results before they are submitted to higher management.

F. Opportunities and Problems

Marketing research reports on an industry, a major market or a line of products usually contain non-proprietary information that is not common knowledge. Having made such a study, a firm can often distribute parts of it to customers and end-users, many of which are smaller firms that might not be able to afford the study. In this way, marketing research results become another form of customer service, therefore another means of product differentiation and a competitive advantage.

Allusion was made in Section C, above, to two common problems of marketing researchers — credibility and image. There is no simple solution. No official pronouncement from the Chief Executive Officer can make a skeptical client believe the findings of a researcher he feels is inexperienced or biased. Not even the appointment as Marketing Research Manager of a successful and respected former sales representative or manufacturing area superintendent will necessarily convince him. Usually, the only solution is a mounting record of successful performance over a period of time. The process can be accelerated by arranging frequent contacts between researchers and clients, on the job and off; e.g., by having the researcher visit customers with sales representatives, participate in sales meetings, report his results in product program review meetings, play golf with personnel of other divisions at picnics, "socialize" at division cocktail parties, etc.

Another problem is in communication, both oral and written. Marketing research reports should be presented lucidly and tersely (see Chapter 3), with an absolute minimum of jargon. Great care should be taken to avoid parochial applications of terminology; for example, the term "business research" means corporate planning to some companies, venture evaluation to others, and organizational auditing to still others. If misinterpretation is likely, a glossary of terms should be used.

QUESTIONS

1. In selecting persons for assignment to marketing research, what are the advantages and disadvantages of picking (1) a marketing employee who has an interest in working with numbers, (2) a management scientist?

2. If you were a marketing researcher, would you prefer (1) a career assignment, or (2) a "stepping-stone" assignment? Why?

CHAPTER 3

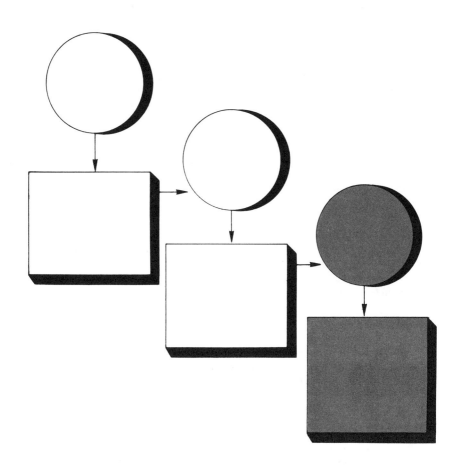

PLANNING, EXECUTING AND REPORTING ASSIGNMENTS

A. Introduction

Whether an assignment is self-generated or is originated by a marketing manager, purchasing agent, company president or some other client, there are rules to be observed, hazards to be avoided and procedures to be followed for optimum results.

For illustration, the case of a descriptive study involving a field survey is employed here.

B. Problem Definition

The real problem may be more complex than it appears to be at first. A marketing manager who looks at his latest sales report and asks why sales are below (or above) forecast in one territory may set into motion an inquiry that can not be completed without investigating trends in the national economy, in public opinion, in product or service improvements by his competitors or the morale of his field sales force.

Therefore, a marketing researcher should not accept a short statement or simple question at face value and immediately dash out to work. He or she must probe by asking questions about business conditions, competitive trends, customer complaints, etc., until the fundamental problem has been uncovered as well as possible.

The researcher should also learn who is asking for the study, who must approve making the study, who will ultimately use the results of the study, how those results will be used, what kinds of decisions may be based on the results, what the financial consequences may be, when the results must be available to be usable and approximately what expenditures of funds and manpower can be justified in making the study.

Every reasonable effort should be made, at this early stage, to learn *all* of the questions to be answered, for any additional questions raised after the study has been completed will be answerable only by unlikely coincidence.

Finally, the marketing researcher should ascertain the preferred form in which the report is to be made; i.e., memorandum, oral, informal, profile or full formal report.

C. Background Facts

Before searching for new information, marketing researchers should review their files to see if the problem has been encountered and solved in the past. They should then go to the Marketing Information System for available pertinent statistics; and, if appropriate, they should check Field Sales call reports, talk to accounting and planning personnel, and survey all pertinent publications (secondary sources).

D. Confirmation of the Assignment

Formally, and preferably in writing, there should be a clear agreement between the Marketing Research Manager and the client, before the major study is begun.

The letter to the client should define the task, indicate the scope of the study, the use that will be made of the results and the estimated target completion date and cost.

If a consultant can do the job cheaper and/or more quickly or effectively, this is the time to suggest the names of appropriate consulting individuals or firms.

E. Search and Analysis

Details of this phase will be peculiar to each job. Seasoned marketing researchers will need little supervision. Nevertheless, the Marketing Research Manager should show interest, offer advice, suggest sources of information, and at the same time see that the job is progressing on schedule. If the researcher is pressed by concurrent responsibilities, the Manager may have to alter priorities or shift a job to another researcher, temporarily.

A draft of a tentative table of contents for the report should be prepared, first, as a discipline to insure that the researcher has thoroughly visualized the assignment, the information needed and the analysis to be made.

Before embarking upon a field survey, decisions must be made not only about the specific information sought but also about (1) what and how much is to be revealed to respondents of the firm's intentions in making the study, (2) what number and types of firms are to be contacted (customers, distributors, end-users, etc.), (3) whether the survey is to be made by mailed questionnaire, by telephone or by personal interviews, (4) whether one or more researchers must be engaged in the survey, (5) what amount of money, if any, is to be allocated for travel and (6) what number and classes of respondents are to be questioned (purchasing agents, engineers, research chemists, production managers, sales personnel, company officers, etc.).

If customers, potential customers, end-users, distributors and (especially) competitors are to be surveyed, it is important that the study be coordinated with the field sales organization. If suppliers are to be contacted, the purchasing organization should be informed.

Industrial marketing research differs from consumer research in many ways, one of them being that there usually are some genuine experts who know specifically what characteristics a product must have to succeed. Most of these experts usually are willing to help a marketing researcher, because his or her results may be of benefit to the expert and his company.

Finding the experts is sometimes difficult. In some cases, the problem is finding an expert who is authorized to speak for his firm; and it may be necessary, first, to seek out a company officer, manager or purchasing agent, who will give the expert that authority.

There are no invariable rules for choosing surveys by mail vs. telephone vs. personal interview, or for their conduct; but there are these guidelines.

○ *Mailed Questionnaires* are used when (1) there is a very large and/or widely-scattered universe to survey, so that even telephone calling would be prohibitively expensive, (2) only a few, very specific questions are involved (preferably answerable in numbers, by "yes" or "no", or in a few words), and (3) there is little risk that the respondent will misunderstand or misinterpret the questions.

The questionnaire is made easy to answer by providing check-off spaces and multiple choices, if appropriate. Any questions that might be taken as impertinent or a bit too personal are put toward the end in the hope that the respondent will develop an interest in the subject and an empathy with the researcher before he reaches them.

A personalized covering letter should carefully explain the purpose of the survey, state how the results might benefit the respondent, guarantee his anonymity, guarantee non-disclosure of his individual responses and (if feasible) offer him a summary of at least part of the aggregated results. To insure maximum resonse, the letter should be addressed to a particular individual (by name as well as title or function), the questionnaire should avoid confidential information and should be brief, and provision should be made for a follow-up mailing to elicit slow or reluctant responses. The inclusion of money, stamps or other "bribes" should be strictly avoided as inappropriate to a professional relationship; but a self-addressed, stamped return envelope should be enclosed, always.

○ *Telephone Interviews* are useful when the number of respondents is too great to justify travel and/or the questions are relatively few and understandable with little or no explanation. The advantages of telephone over personal interviews are to provide a larger number of contacts within a limited time span and budget, and to simplify the researcher's task of taking notes and recording verbatim responses. The disadvantages are that (1) this method does not accord the interview the same prestige, (2) there is less chance for interaction to assure understanding and to follow unexpected avenues, (3) the communication must be brief and without long explanations, and (4) there is always some risk that the respondent will suddenly terminate the conversation for lack of interest or because he suspects the researcher's motivation, especially if the subject is sensitive and/or the call has been made without prior acquaintance (i.e., a "cold" call).

Whenever possible, respondents should be chosen not only because they have the desired information but also because they are acquaintances or can be approached through sales representatives, other acquaintances or some common interest, such as membership in a professional society, fraternity, service club or trade association. It may be appropriate to pre-notify a very busy respondent, thus giving him the opportunity to look up data and to suggest a convenient time for a more leisurely telephone interview.

As in the mail questionnaire, the researcher must explain the purpose of his survey and make sure that the respondent sees a benefit in cooperating. After each question, he must *listen* — not suggest answers, not lead the discussion, but listen. Of course, he should not silently accept an answer that seems to derive from a misunderstanding of the question: he should probe diplomatically, remembering that to argue may bring a premature end to the interview.

The conversation should be closed with a request for permission to call again if the researcher's notes prove to be incomplete or confusing, and with a warm expression of gratitude for the respondent's time and helpfulness.

○ *Personal Interviews* are used whenever time and budget permit thorough coverage of a subject. They permit maximum interaction, explanation and probing, not only for facts and figures but also for opinions, conjectures, projections and wishes.

The researcher must study the subject beforehand to prepare the most pertinent and provocative questions, to present a posture of modest expertise and to insure that he not only will understand the responses but also will detect and pursue any leads to unexpected and worthwhile supplementary intelligence.

All of the interviews with the preferred prospective respondents should be by appointment, made well in advance and scheduled to allow enough time for a comfortable, but not wasteful discussion. Geography permitting, three or four interviews can be accomplished in a full day; but a half-hour gap between the end of one and the beginning of the next is not just insurance against being late; it provides a golden opportunity to review and augment notes. Alternative stops in the vicinity should have been located in advance for cold calls, in case a scheduled interview is aborted because the respondent has suddenly been called out of town or into a conference.

Although finding the expert respondent in a customer's organization should be relatively easy because of the established relationship, certain protocol must be observed.

1. Sales personnel should be consulted, in most firms, before marketing researchers visit their customers. The salesman or saleswoman may want to pre-notify the intended respondent and to be present during the interview. If he or she knows the customer well, finding the expert(s) will be greatly facilitated, and the interview(s) should proceed smoothly and productively. (There may be a rare occasion on which relations with a customer have been jeopardized by friction, misunderstanding, late delivery or a credit problem, causing the salesman to veto a proposed interview or to insist on handling it personally, perhaps in the absence of the researcher. All reasonable efforts should be made, including appeal to appropriate sales management by the researcher's client, to get the researcher in with authorization to proceed, diplomatically.)

2. In many customer calls, Purchasing is the "front door", even if the desired expert is in another division, as the first contact is expected to be made through Purchasing, as a matter of courtesy. Furthermore, the purchasing agent can help identify and contact the expert(s), and is usually glad to do so, especially if he has been convinced that the study may lead to better products and services for him and his employer.

In trying to arrange for an interview, there is no better way to establish a friendly relationship than by being open and frank about the objectives, the reasons behind the study, and its possible benefits to both the respondent and the supplier.

An informal atmosphere is almost always best for personal interviews, if it can be managed. Researchers should preferably take few, if any, notes until the interview is over and they have withdrawn to the parking lot or elsewhere. If notes are unavoidable because of the volume of numerical data, etc., they should be taken as casually as possible (but never surreptitiously), after asking permission of the respondent.[1] The use of a tape recorder is definitely *not* encouraged, as it may result in stilted and restrained responses, lacking in imagination, creative thinking and forecasts.

---

[1] On the other hand, some respondents are flattered by copious note-taking.

Marketing researchers should let the discussion wander occasionally to encourage free expression of ideas, to maintain informality, and to be polite. However, they should also bring it back to any important aspect that may have been ignored or incompletely covered. If, in a group of respondents, two conflicting opinions surface, an attempt should be made to learn why there is disagreement. Also, the reasons behind an estimate may be more important than the numbers. As in telephone interviews, researchers must listen, absorb and digest, talking only enough to keep the interview productive.

A respondent who seems reluctant to commit himself to firm statements or speculate on facts and forecasts can often be drawn out if the researcher produces a table or graph and asks for the respondent's evaluation. Even if the respondent only suggests that a number is "far too high", he may be more helpful than otherwise.

Unless the discussion was completely sterile, marketing researchers should suggest the possibility of follow-up by telephone, to ask a question that may have been overlooked or to clarify confusion that may be discovered in their notes.

In some cases, a cooperative respondent may be offered a copy of the intended report, or an informal summary of that portion of direct interest to his company. Whether this is offered or not, he should again be assured that his replies should help the supplier serve his firm better in the future, and he should be offered reciprocal cooperation on any study his firm might undertake.

As the results of the search (by mail, phone or personal interview) accumulate, the marketing researcher should begin the analysis, comparing responses for similarities, trends, inconsistencies and unexpected results. He or she should isolate emerging facts from opinions, compare them with any preconceived ideas, and locate subjects that need clarification. Doubtful areas can be explored in greater depth, and previous respondents can be telephoned to clarify them. This is also the time to consider whether or not to extend the search beyond the initial limits.

If the responses, for example, should indicate that a market is significantly larger or smaller than is shown in published data, accuracy might be questioned and checked by some other means (e.g., by comparing end-use data against processor data). Even official government data should not always be accepted at face value, because they are known to be inaccurate or incomplete in some cases.

Jumping to conclusions or taking an "easy" conclusion can be hazardous, so a researcher should keep an open mind until all the responses are in. At the same time, he or she should not extend the search unduly or over-analyze the data. There is always a deadline to be met.

F. Reporting Results

Good reports, in marketing research as elsewhere, must be timely, pertinent and understandable. An admittedly incomplete study, submitted in time to be used, is far more acceptable than a polished report submitted too late.

The message should be lucidly and tersely expressed in short sentences, with little or no marketing research jargon. If the fine points of technique must be recorded, they should be put into an appendix.

As in all business reports, the introduction, summary, conclusions and recommendations should come first, so that the busiest executives will find it easy to read at least that much. Charts and graphs should be attractive, clear and simple, but painstakingly accurate.

A cardinal rule is "Avoid surprising or embarassing your client". Normally, the researcher will keep his or her client advised of progress during the study, pointing out any unexpected findings, especially if they are contrary to the client's favorite opinions. The client should be offered an oral report before the written report has been typed, in case more work should be requested; and copies of the written report should go to the client before they are released to higher management. This enables the client to read the report before some superior can call and ask questions.

The warnings of the preceding paragraph should not be interpreted as implying that a client should be allowed to alter the facts or conclusions of a study. His contrary opinion might be cited in the report; but Marketing Research must be objective or it will lose credibility.

A conscientious marketing researcher will not distribute a final report and then forget it. He or she will follow up, a few weeks or months later, to see if the results are being used. If they are not, inquiry will be made to learn if the report was misunderstood, unconvincing or moot because of some shift in business or the economy. Learning from mistakes is painful, but the lessons so taught are usually well remembered and beneficial. If the results were well received, implemented and successful, the report can be used as evidence of expertise when the time comes to market the services of the Marketing Research Section to another potential client.

QUESTION

Imagine you are a marketing researcher for a maker of shipping containers, and you have been assigned to interview key customers to ascertain any needs they may foresee for containers of a different size, shape, construction, etc. What questions would you ask, and in what sequence?

CHAPTER 4

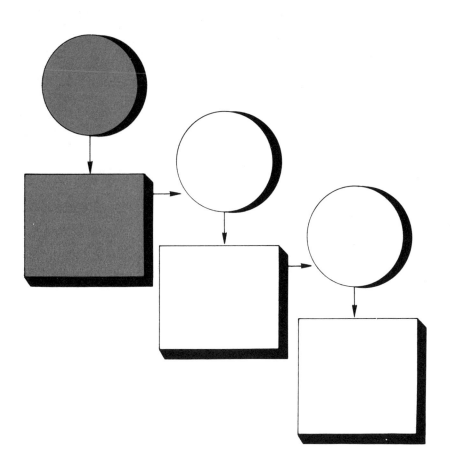

IDENTIFYING MARKETS AND COMPANIES

A. Objectives

Nobody sells to a vacuum. Few can afford to wait for customers to come to them. No supplier can intelligently invest in plants, schedule production and move his goods to customers without knowing his markets.

Knowing the markets means much more than just knowing the probable demand in units or dollars. It means knowing what is expected in the way of product attributes, product line assortment, pricing level and structure, terms of sale, personal selling, distribution and delivery. It means knowing how the market is segmented, what degree of product differentiation is required and what amount of diversification might be beneficial. It means knowing the markets intimately.

Marketing people need to know who are their current and potential customers, end-users and competitors. They need to know what products these firms make and to whom they sell, what they buy and from whom. They ought to know as much as possible about their business policies and practices.

With such knowledge,

o marketing researchers can identify markets and proceed to measure and project demand, sales and prices

o marketing management can plan and implement appropriate marketing strategy and tactics

o field salesmen can serve current customers with greater understanding of their business aims, self-images and product needs

o field salesmen can approach potential customers with greater probability of making a sale than would be true if they were blindly knocking on every factory door in the territory (a practice commonly called "smoke-stacking" or "bird-dogging")

o research and development managers can use the information to develop projects and guide programs.

Identification reports (i.e., reports that identify and describe markets and companies) contain many quantitative data, but tend to be mainly qualitative. They usually contain information gathered from both

o *primary sources:* that is, customers, end-users and other individuals

o *secondary sources:* such as directories, trade publications, government reports, and consultants' studies.

They vary in complexity from a simple but selective prospect list for salesmen; to profiles of current and potential customers, end-users and competitors; to a comprehensive description of the industries comprising the market for a product or product line.

B. Company Profiles

The descriptive information for a profile may include

o company name, location(s), principal activities, principal products and any geographical limits on marketing efforts

○ names of principal officers, directors, owners, parent company and/or subsidiaries (if any), principal suppliers and principal customers
○ size, as measured by assets, revenues, production capacities, producing units,
   sales in units or dollars (by major product lines), market share(s) and/or
   number of employees
○ financial strength, credit rating, growth trend, and capital spending for new
   capacity and modernization
○ pricing policy and tactics
○ sales and profit growth rates
○ history of diversification and/or product differentiation (including aban-
   donment of obsolete or unprofitable items), source of innovations (internal R
   & D vs. licensing vs. acquisition or merger), and probability that past trends
   will continue, shift, accelerate
○ reputation for quality of product and service, and for integrity in negotiating
   and implementing contracts and other agreements
○ corporate policies, especially toward suppliers and competitors
○ business acumen, judgment, trustworthiness and circumspection.

The bulk of this information usually can be found in *secondary sources* (i.e.,
published) such as company prospectuses and annual reports to stockholders and to
the Securities and Exchange Commission ("10K" reports)[2], *Moody's Industrials,
Value Line* and other investment house publications, government publications such
as the *Minerals Yearbook,* certain trade association periodicals and annual statistical
compilations, various directories of associations, and descriptive feature articles
from *Fortune, Business Week, The Wall Street Journal* and other business publications.[3] For privately held companies, the only secondary sources may be credit
reports such as the Dun and Bradstreet service and consultant studies.

The gaps left by secondary sources must be filled in by going to *primary sources,*
especially for subjective materials. The best primary source will be, of course, an
officer of the company whose profile is being prepared. Most customers and end-
users are quite willing to cooperate if they have been told how the profile will help
the supplier guide his efforts to provide better products and services for them. Even
future thinking on expansion and company aims may be revealed if they see this as
a way to help assure ample supplies of adequate raw materials, improved components or specially designed equipment.

Competitors, naturally, are more reticent, but even they may reveal clues to
policy, organization and strategy in the course of a relaxed conversation in an
informal atmosphere.

As a means of cross-checking useful information about one customer or competitor may be obtained by questioning other customers and/or competitors.

Some of the most important items in this list can be derived only by astute
observation and seasoned judgment. To get these, the marketing researcher should
supplement his information with the opinions of his firm's salesmen, field sales

---

[2] Both stockholders' and 10K reports can usually be obtained by writing to the company's
Secretary.
[3] See Giragosian, *Chemical Marketing Research,* Reinhold, 1967, Chapter 4 for a comprehensive listing by source, type and market. Also, Heskett, *Marketing,* Macmillan, 1976, Appendix
A, pp. 545–576.

managers, purchasing department and headquarters managerial personnel. Salesmen's call reports and various internal company files make a good beginning, but the more confidential and controversial judgmental material probably will not have been recorded.

Good judgment must be exercised in deciding which customers, end-users or competitors are important enough to be profiled thoroughly, which should be sketched only roughly and which should be merely listed by name, location and some measure of size.

An example of a company profile is given in Appendix A.

C. Industry Descriptions

The market for a line of industrial goods usually consists of several industries. These may be defined according to their products, processes or technologies; for example, the automotive industry (product), the die-casting industry (process), and the electronics industry (technology).

In preparing a comprehensive industry description, a marketing researcher may include

- o a careful definition of the industry and a summary statement of its significance (e.g., annual dollar purchases or sales)
- o segmentation of the industry by major and minor product groupings, process or technological variations, raw materials utilized and/or corporate affiliations (e.g., custom vs. captive vs. proprietary plastics molding shops)
- o a listing of the major and minor firms in the industry and their inter-relations, if any, through formal corporate ties or supplier-purchaser practices
- o some historical background to assist understanding of the industry's status and trade practices
- o at least a sketchy description of the products made, the processes and equipment used and trends in technology, economic plant size and profitability
- o all the available useful data on capacities, production, consumption, investments, revenues and profits, by segment and by firm, for several years in the recent past, with industry projections into the future
- o quantitative data on trends in past purchases, and a qualitative picture of processor technology trends and end-user preferences, especially if these might significantly alter processors' purchasing patterns in the future
- o any pertinent information on competitive threats to the industry from radically different, substitute products or new end-user technologies that might render its present products obsolete
- o a very careful analysis of the exact performance characteristics the industry really wants in the materials, components, supplies or equipment it requires vs. those now being supplied, and an estimate of the market share that might be captured by the supplier who devised and offered a new product that met *all* the requirements better or fully
- o the marketing researcher's best forecast of the industry's total demand and his firm's probable sales in the next several years (see Chapter 4 for methods)
- o the marketing researcher's best estimate of the prices the industry will be

paying for his firm's goods in the next several years (see Chapter 5 for methods)

○ a careful appraisal of the market shares now enjoyed by his firm's competitors, with any indications of trends in those market shares and the reasons for the trends.

Admittedly, such a comprehensive description would not be possible in many cases. It would be unusual if all the information were available. Furthermore, some marketing managers might not feel the results would be worth the time and cost of research, analysis and interpretation. Accordingly, the marketing researcher approaching such an assignment should first ascertain just how much detail really is desired (see Chapter 3).

An industry description containing all this information would be of most interest to top management, marketing managers and product managers. For sales managers, district sales managers and field salesmen, some of the more general sections might be superfluous; hence, it might be desirable to extract for them only the sections specific to their customers and potential customers.

An example of an industry description is given in Appendix B.

D. Identification Reports by Consultants

Some of the best identification reports in existence have been prepared by consultants. They tend to be more objective, and they may be more complete because of the consultant's neutral position with respect to competitors.

E. Putting Significance into Identification Reports

The real importance of a company profile or an industry description lies in the extent to which it answers the question, "What does this mean to *our* company?" Thus, an industry description and a customer (or potential customer) profile should define as accurately as possible the products that the supplier has sold, and/or might sell in the future, to that industry or company. Both quantitative and qualitative (i.e., product types) data are important. Otherwise, the reaction of marketing management may be, "So what?".

Similarly, a competitor profile must assess strengths, weaknesses and apparent trends that might have significant impact on the supplier's market share position and progress.

QUESTIONS AND EXERCISES

1. Compare the content of the Roxco profile (Appendix A) with the information items listed in Section B. What items are missing? How important are they? How could the missing information be obtained?

2. Compare the content of the plastics industry description (Appendix B) with the information items listed in Section C. What items are missing? How important are they? How could the missing information be obtained? Which of the missing items do you think would be worth the search?

3. Pick an industry and a product or service it utilizes. The product may be a

material, a component, a supply (such as cutting oil, wiping rags, floor wax) or a piece of equipment. Prepare an industry description as you would write it if you were a marketing researcher for the supplier of that product or service.

4. Pick a company and a product or service it provides. Write a company profile, assuming it is your competitor.

CHAPTER 5

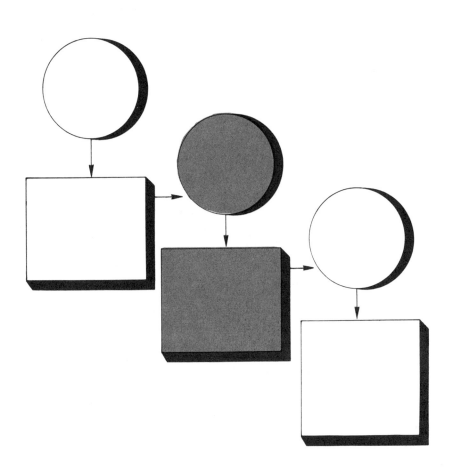

MEASURING CURRENT DEMAND

A. The Importance of a Number

Current demand is a fundamental and vital quantity. It is used by a participating supplier as the basis for calculating his share of a market. It is of interest to a prospective supplier, as he must decide whether or not the market is large enough to warrant the risk of entry. A prospective new user must compare supply with demand to judge whether or not he will find an adequate supply.

In addition, current demand is the base point for forecasting future demand.

B. Estimating Current Demand

If the market of interest is very large, the task of estimating demand may already have been done for us by some government agency, trade association or other organization.

Total shipments for large aggregates of raw materials, machinery and certain supplies are published monthly by the Department of Commerce in *Survey of Current Business, Business Conditions Digest* and *Current Industrial Reports.* Annual figures may be found in the biennial supplement, *Business Statistics,* and in the *Statistical Abstract of the United States.* (See Giragosian, Chapter 4 for complete list of sources.) The U.S. International Trade Commission (formerly Tariff Commission) collects and publishes data on thousands of chemicals in "Synthetic Organic Chemicals, U.S. Production and Sales". Similar statistics are compiled by trade associations, such as The Society of the Plastics Industry, 355 Lexington Ave., New York, N.Y., 10017. Many trade magazines, such as *Modern Plastics,* publish annual and some monthly estimates.

Demand data for *segments* of these large aggregates are not usually available and must be estimated. Generally, the smaller the segment, the greater the difficulty we will have in making an estimate. For example, given published data on polystyrene resins for injection molding, we probably could estimate the demand for pigmented resins with acceptable accuracy after asking several experienced marketing people for their estimates of the percentage distribution between crystal and colored resin.

However, to estimate demand for very narrow segments, it may be necessary to send marketing researchers or others into the field to collect data from processors or end-users. For example, a major supplier of plastics resins has sent technologists armed with laboratory balances into molding shops to weigh gears,levers and other molded parts. Knowing the weight per part and the number of parts used annually in specific automobiles, appliances, telephones and other end-products, the supplier was able to estimate demand for his resins in very narrow market segments.

In some cases, only an indirect estimate seems feasible. We may have to estimate demand for the product of interest from the known or estimated demand for something else. Imagine we were trying to estimate demand for a chemical used as an additive, a colorant or a catalyst in the manufacture of synthetic rubber latex. We might find the only approach would be to find published data for total latex, estimate the fraction that is of interest to us (e.g.. water-base coatings), and ascertain the average concentration or requirement for the additive. colorant or catalyst.

From all of these, we could estimate the annual demand for, say, peroxide catalysts in a certain class of synthetic rubber latex.

Even more indirectly, some demand data can be estimated best from a knowledge of the capacity of a consuming industry. Suppose we knew which foundries made die-cast parts for certain toys. We might learn or estimate how many machines each used, the capacities of the machines and the average number of months per year the machines were in operation making toy parts. Making reasonable allowances for machine down-time, average productivity, percentage yield of usable castings, scrap loss and so on, we could estimate the consumption of zinc or other die-casting alloy demanded for the annual production of those toys.

Naturally, we would feel more confident if we weighed the cast parts and multiplied by the number of toys produced. But toy manufacturers are most reluctant to reveal data of possible interest to competitors.

Perhaps the most indirect and least reliable estimate is that made from employment numbers. Various business services, notably *Dun's Market Identifiers,* offer a large collection of data, including SIC number and number of employees, on thousands of plants, factories, warehouses and offices. By selecting the appropriate processors and summing the numbers of production employees, one can estimate demand for goods assuming he has a reasonable estimate of consumption per employee.

C. Cross-Checking for Accuracy

Estimates of demand should be checked, if at all practical, for error, exaggeration, duplication and omission. An estimate for a market involving several industries should be examined, industry by industry (i.e., segment by segment) for reasonableness. Estimates of demand by a group of processors (e.g., abrasives manufacturers) should be cross-checked by totaling consumption by end-users (e.g., firms that grind, polish, de-burr, etc. shapes and articles of metal, ceramic, wood, plastics, etc.)

Cross-checking should be done by different forms of segmentation, where possible, also; for example, by geography (e.g., sales territory), by industry, and/or by end-use.

Even government statistics are only as good as the reports from individual sources; and all too often, the clerk making a report has no reason to see or use the final published aggregate, does not truly understand the technical definitions of product categories, and considers the report he must make an irritating chore to be delayed as long as possible and to be done with least acceptable effort, if at all.

Consultants can be very helpful (see Chapter 2, Section E) in estimating demand. A multi-client study or service containing the necessary data, already published or soon to be released, would be relatively inexpensive. Even a special study may save money and time, and the consultant's expertise and neutrality may provide access to data and a degree of accuracy not otherwise obtainable.

QUESTIONS AND EXERCISES

1. Input-output tables, such as those published by the U.S. Department of Commerce[1] relate supply by one industry to another. How can these data be used to estimate current demand? What are the limitations of this approach?

2. Pick an industrial product or service and estimate recent demand by some market segment, from published data. Document your sources, and justify any intuitive manipulation of the published data needed to derive demand for your chosen segment of the total market.

[1] *Survey of Current Business,* November 1969, pp. 30—43.

CHAPTER 6

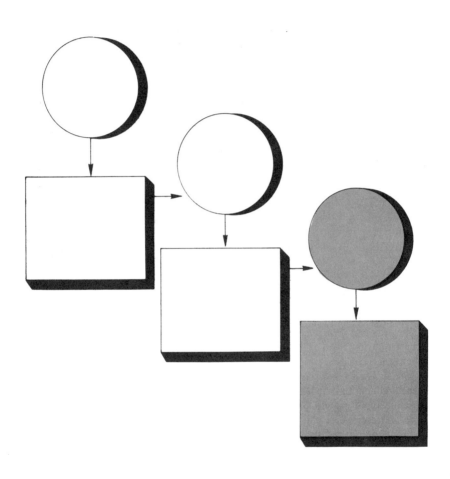

ESTIMATING FUTURE DEMAND

A. Art or Science?

Forecasting is both art *and* science. Sometimes, it is mostly art — or to be more precise, it is largely a matter of good judgment.

B. Forecasting Methods.

Forecasts can be classified most usefully according to the method used. In addition to purely intuitive forecasts by an individual or by a "jury of experts", there are at least four main types
- Built-up
- Naive
- Econometric (top-down)
- Opportunistic

C. Built-up Forecast

As the name implies, this forecast is the result of summing estimates for market segments to get a total. For a supplier's sales forecast, the segments usually are geographical, and the procedure commonly begins with each salesman's forecast for his territory. If sales are made to several industries, the summation may require collecting territory estimates from two or more sales forces serving different market segments. Usually, these figures are edited by district sales managers, regional sales managers and finally the national sales manager as each makes adjustments to reflect his broader and more mature perspective. The forecast may be for total market demand, for a single supplier's sales, or for both.

The resulting total is a collective judgment based on a very detailed examination of the market, customer by customer. It has built into it each customer's knowledge or anticipation of his commitments for future delivery. These, in turn, reflect expectations of the end-users.

The advantages of the built-up forecast are derived from this microscopic approach which anticipates the effects of each significant event; for example, the probable rapid growth of a successful new end-product, the up-coming completion of an end-user's new plant, the cancellation of a government contract, the instrusion of a replacement product or the gradual death of an obsolescent product, process or technology.

It has four more or less serious disadvantages.
- It may be high because salesmen tend to be optimists
- It may be low if salesmen have real or fancied reasons for shading the goals that may be set for them
- It may be high if several processors each expect to be awarded all or a major part of a large supply contract
- It may not adequately take into account the trends of the business cycle.

Nevertheless, a built-up forecast usually is the most accurate *short-term* sales forecast. And it may also be the best short-term forecast of industry demand, if the salesmen really know their market shares. What length of time is meant by short-term varies among industries, but it usually means a year or less.

Built-up forecasts of total industry demand are frequently made from estimates of future consumption by processor category and by end-use (another type of segmentation; see Chapter 1, Section A and Chapter 5, Sections B and C), using figures from processors and/or end-users. They enjoy much the same advantages and disadvantages as other built-up forecasts.

D. Naive Forecast

A forecast extrapolated entirely from past data for industry consumption or supplier sales is called a naive forecast. The term does not imply that it is blind or stupid, but only that it assumes a continuation of the past, including growth or declining trends in total or in market share.

Basically, the method is a simple regression of sales or total demand against time. This may be done graphically or analytically, with or without a computer. A simple analytical tool is the "least squares" method described below, to get a straight line having the equation,

$$Y_T = a + b \, X, \qquad \text{Equation } 6-1$$

in which Y_T is sales or demand, X is time, a and b are constants.

Let us assume, for illustration, that we have these tabulated data (see Table 6–1) for annual sales (Y values) and that we assign arbitrary numbers (X values) for the years.

Table 6–1.

Year	Y	X	X²	XY
1971	2,099	−2	4	−4198
1972	2,390	−1	1	−2390
1973	2,296	0	0	0
1974	2,186	+1	1	+2186
1975	2,529	+2	4	+5058
Σ	11,500	0	10	+ 656

We then calculate the constants, a and b, from the equations,

$$a = \Sigma \, Y/N = 11{,}500 \div 5 = 2{,}300$$

$$b = \Sigma \, XY/\Sigma \, X^2 = 656 \div 10 = 66$$

where N is the number of years for which we have sales figures.

$$\text{Therefore, } Y_T = 2{,}300 + 66\,X \qquad\qquad \text{Equation 6-2}$$

Projecting forward to 1976, for which X = 3, we would forecast sales of

$$Y_T = 2{,}300 + 66 \times 3 = 2500. \qquad\qquad \text{Equation 6-3}$$

We use the subscript T for this forecast to indicate that it is based on the so-called *secular trend*, without correction for the business cycle or for seasonality. Later, in Section G of this Chapter, we will consider those corrections.

Notice that this method of forecasting assumes a constant increment of growth each year; i.e., an increase of 66 (units or value). For some products, growth tends to be more nearly exponential, and it would be more appropriate to calculate the *growth rate*; e.g., 9.3% per year.

To illustrate, let us take the data of Table 6-2 as another example.

Table 6-2.

Year	Y
1971	8,500
1972	9,100
1973	10,500
1974	11,800
1975	12,200

We want to derive the constants, a and n, in the equation

$$Y_T = a\,(1+n)^X \qquad\qquad \text{Equation 6-4}$$

where X is the number of years from some base year, a is the calculated sales volume in the base year, and n is the growth rate (expressed as a decimal fraction).

As in the previous calculation a computer program would give a precise and quick solution. We can also use a combination graphical-analytical method, which is just as quick. It is accurate enough for our purposes, when we admit that no naive forecast of sales is likely to be closer than ±5%, unless we are dealing with a large aggregate.

Plotting sales against time gives us the solid black points in Figure 6-1, and we draw a line through them, as shown. We pick coordinates for two points, one near each end of the line, to use in calculating the growth rate, n. Notice that actual data points, such as the figure 8500 for the year 1971 should *not* be used unless they happen to fall on the line.

Using the points indicated by small open squares, we have values of

14,100 at 1976 and
7,600 at 1970.

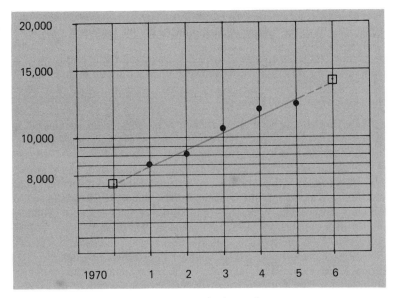

Figure 6—1. Annual sales vs. time.

If we count time in years from 1970, these values substituted in Equation 6—4 give

$$14,100 = a (1 + n)^6$$
$$7,600 = a (1 + n)^0,$$

from which it follows that a = 7,600 and

$$14,100 = 7,600 (1 + n)^6$$
$$\frac{14,100}{7,600} = 1.86 = (1 + n)^6$$
$$(1.86)^{1/6} = 1 + n = 1.11$$

Then, n = 0.11, indicating an average 11% per year growth rate, and our equation for forecasting is

$$Y_T = 7,600 (1.11)^X, \qquad \text{Equation 6—5}$$

with which we could estimate sales for 1977 to be $7,600 (1.11)^7 = 15,400$.

It must be admitted that the sales figures obtained from this equation are hardly more accurate than could be obtained by purely graphical extension of the line in Figure 6—1. However, the equation is worth deriving, if only to obtain the growth rate.

The advantages of the naive forecast are simplicity, speed and the demonstrable facts on which it is based. The disadvantages are that

o it ignores any influences of changes in customers' and competitors' activities

○ it ignores any influences of major changes in the supplier's own marketing effort and strategy

○ it ignores effects of the business cycle and broad economic trends

○ it can never, by definition, show a turning point, either up or down.

E. Econometric (Top-Down) Forecast

For a long time, it has been recognized that demand for a particular product or product line is related to demand for one or more large aggregates. The demand for industrial finishes necessarily depends, in the long run, on the demand for automobiles, refrigerators, office and residential furniture, and many other end-products. Therefore, it is logical to estimate demand for a product from published economic indicators, such as the Federal Reserve Board (FRB) Index of Durable Manufacturers, Disposable Personal Income, Construction Contracts, production of automobiles, major appliances, electrical machinery and so on.

Selecting the most appropriate indicators takes good judgment, great care and often considerable patience. We should consider three classes of indicators

○ **product aggregate**; that is, the group of products including the product we are trying to forecast (e.g., electrical machinery manufactures, if we are forecasting demand for electrical motor switches)

○ **direct derivative aggregate**; that is, a group of intermediate products at least one of which is expected to be made from the product we are trying to forecast (e.g., laminated sheeting production, if we are forecasting demand for an adhesive)

○ **end-product aggregate**; that is, a group of final products at least one of which would be an end-use for the product we are trying to forecast (e.g., home appliances, if we are forecasting demand for a pigment used in baking enamels).

As a first step, we ought to search for indicators in all three classes, and should try various combinations of them in our exploratory regression analyses.

To predict the demand for copper, we might logically consider the FRB index of metal mining (parent aggregate), the production quantities or indexes for wire and cable and for sheet, pipe and tubing (direct derivatives) and production quantities or indexes for industrial construction, electrical machinery, electric power transmission and residential construction (end-use markets).

The difficulty with this approach in the past was a lack of forecast values for the indicators. Only straight-line projections were available, usually. But we now have several very sophisticated and gigantic models of the economy,[1] programmed to include expected effects of tax, tariff and other legislation, restraints on interest rates and money supply, etc. With the economic indicators forecast by these models, we can proceed with more confidence to develop top-down, or econometric forecasts, recognizing however, that even these models are not perfect, especially several years into the future.

---

[1] Such as those of the Brookings Institution, Wharton School, the University of Michigan, Chase Econometrics Associates, Data Resources, Inc., and the National Bureau of Economic Research.

We want an expression of the form

$$Y_T = a + b\,I_b + c\,I_c + d\,I_d + \cdots \qquad \text{Equation 6-6}$$

in which a, b, c, d — are constants (coefficients) and I_b, I_c, I_d — are economic indicators. To get it, we start with data such as those of table 6-3.

Table 6-3.

Year	Demand	I_b	I_c	I_d	I_e
1965	391	115.9	685	9,335	473
1966	537	134.4	750	9,988	512
1967	703	148.4	794	10,721	547
1968	817	144.4	866	11,458	590
1969	950	158.7	930	11,863	634
1970	1082	156.6	976	13,352	690
1971	1257	158.6	1060	13,736	744
1972	1486	148.2	1155	14,523	797
1973	1774	140.5	1289	15,441	883

A computer program is used for multiple regression of the dependent variable (sales or demand) against the independent variables (economic indicators). From it, we get not only the coefficients a, b, c, d — but also their standard errors, the partial coefficients of determination, the coefficient of multiple determination and usually one or more measures of significance, such as the Durbin-Watson statistics, the standard error of the estimate, the t-ratios and the F-test values.[2]

Let us suppose that our computer gave us Equation 6-7 as the result of regression.

$$Y_T = -1272 + 0.73\,I_b + 0.027\,I_c - 1.86\,I_d + 0.12\,I_e \qquad \text{Equation 6-7}$$

If the multiple coefficient of determination, R^2, were at least 0.85, we would probably be quite encouraged, as this would indicate that our equation accounts for 85% of the variations in sales.

Suppose, however, that partial coefficients of determination or t-values indicated that I_c contributed very little to the result. In the interest of always keeping our equation as simple as possible,[3] and of minimizing the effort required to use it (and, incidentally, minimizing the chance of introducing keypunching errors), we should run the regression again, eliminating I_c. Let us say this gave us Equation 6-8

$$Y_T = -1296 + 0.77\,I_b - 1.43\,I_d + 0.15\,I_e \qquad \text{Equation 6-8}$$

[2] For discussions of significance tests, see specialized books, such as Richmond, S. B., *Statistical Analysis*, The Ronald Press Co., 1964.

[3] "Most statisticians subscribe to the law of parsimony, which dictates the use of the simplest possible model or theory to explain a given problem", Buzzel, Cox and Brown, *Marketing Research and Information Systems*. McGraw-Hill, 1969, p. 187.

for which R^2 was 0.88. This would be an improvement in accountability as well as in simplicity.

There is, however, one serious shortcoming in both Equations 6–7 and 6–8. This is the negative sign of the coefficient by which I_d is multiplied. Mathematically, the sign is correct and the equations necessarily fit the data better because of it. But practically speaking, the negative sign means that Y_T varies *inversely* with I_d.

If, for example, our expression related the demand for aluminum extruded shapes with such indicators as housing completions, appliance production, lighting fixture sales and investments in plant and equipment, one would expect demand to vary directly, not inversely, with each of the indicators. That very expectation would, in fact, have been the reason for trying the regression with those particular indicators.

So, if the marketing researcher takes the results of his forecast to his marketing manager or product manager, he can expect a very skeptical reception if the "best" equation says, in effect, that demand drops as appliance production rises. The pragmatic business man who has asked for the forecast knows that he sells aluminum extrusions to appliance makers, and he is most unlikely to be impressed by arguments for "mathematical neatness" if the expression is illogical.

In such a case, we should first have experimented with regression against only I_b and I_e, or with I_b and I_e and some new indicator I_f, until we found an equation that was both acceptably accurate and logical.

Most econometric forecasts utilize coincident indicators rather than leading or lagging indicators as the independent variables. To forecast sales of a product with a long lead time, such as switches for nuclear power plants, one might use either

○ a leading indicator or

○ a forecast value of a coincident indicator.

Having derived the equation that best satisfies our mathematical and pragmatic criteria, we are prepared to forecast future sales and/or demand. We obtain projected future values for our economic indicators from a model of the economy, insert them into the equation and calculate the forecast(s).

The first and most important advantage of an econometric forecast is that it is logically derived from the known relation of a product to its industry aggregate, to its derivative markets and/or to its end-use markets. Secondly, it should correctly include the influences of major industrial trends and the economic cycle, including turning points, if it employs indicators predicted by a comprehensive model of the economy. It is, therefore, probably the best long-range (2–10 year) forecasting method.

Its major disadvantage is that it does not include the effects of anticipated changes at the micro level; that is, changes in the marketing effectiveness of the supplier and in the activities of his customers and competitors.

Occasionally, a marketing researcher may succeed in deriving an econometric forecasting equation of outstanding historical accuracy only to discover that there are no available predictions of one or more key independent variables. If he can not predict them himself, he must be content to use a less accurate version.

F. Opportunistic Forecast

When a marketing researcher modifies his naive or econometric forecast by combining it with his expectations of changes at the micro level, the result is an opportunistic forecast. He uses all the information he can get from all sources, including his best judgment, thereby increasing its accuracy, both short- and long-range.

Some years ago, when I was a marketing research manager, one of my "clients" was a sales manager who regularly required a built-up forecast from his field sales force and an independent, econometric forecast from Marketing Research. Placing the two forecasts on his desk, he then combined them with his own judgment into an opportunistic forecast that he was willing to submit to top management.

Especially in the case of very long-term forecasts (10 to 50 years), consideration must be given to the possible impacts of trends in the economy, technological developments, availability of raw materials and political, sociological, cultural and life-style influences. Most major changes of this nature can be anticipated because they usually occur gradually. Many sophisticated techniques for visualizing such trends, assessing their probabilities and estimating their influences have been explored in the last 15 or 20 years.[4] Notable among these are cross-impact analysis, KSIM, dynamic models and policy capture. Most of them require teams of experts and more time and money than can be justified except by large companies and government agencies.

Table 6–4 gives comparisons of the advantages and disadvantages of various forecasting methods.

G. Corrections for Cycle and Seasonality

Some markets seem to have a cyclical variation, more or less independent of broad economic trends; for example, the textile business. If this is known or suspected, its effect can usually be estimated and applied as a correction to the forecast.

To estimate the cyclical correction, we compare actual historical sales or demand, Y, with the calculated figures, Y_T, for the same years, from our forecast equation (either naive or econometric). For example, we might take the Y values of Table 6–1, calculate the Y_T values from Equation 6–2, and compare them as in Table 6–5.

With so few data, we can not be sure; but it would appear that there is a cycle, with perhaps a three year period from peak to peak, in which the trough is about 0.94 and the peak about 1.05 times the straight-line predicted value (see Figure 6–2). From this, we might assume that our forecast for 1976 would be fairly accurate without correction, but that our forecast for 1977 should be reduced 6% for the cyclical effect.[5]

---

[4] Mitchell, Dodge, Kruzic, Miller, Schwartz and Suta, *Handbook of Forecasting Methods,* Stanford Research Institute, 1975, pp. 103–186.
[5] See the works of Jay W. Forrester, especially *Industrial Dynamics,* The M.I.T. Press, 1961, for more precise methods.

Table 6—4. Comparison of Forecasting Methods.

Type	Advantages	Disadvantages
Built-up	Microscopic approach anticipates effects of anticipated events Good for short term	Depends on judgments of individuals. May include duplication. May ignore trends of economic cycle
Naive	Simple, fast and cheap Based on historical record Fair to good for short term	Ignores changes in customers' and competitors' activities. Ignores effects of supplier's marketing effort Ignores trends of economic cycle Can never predict a turning point
Econometric	Based on known relation to aggregate(s) Can predict turning points Fair to good for long term	Ignores effects of micro events Limited by accuracy of forecasts of aggregate(s)
Opportunistic	Based on all available information Best for both short and long term	Depends partly on judgments of individuals
Cross-Impact etc.	Takes all imaginable future trends into account Probably the only worthwhile approach for very long term	Highly dependent on judgment Costly in funds, manpower and time

Table 6—5.

Year	Actual (Y)	Calculated (Y_T)	Cyclical Correction (Y/Y_T)
1971	2099	2168	0.97
1972	2390	2234	1.07
1973	2296	2300	1.00
1974	2186	2366	0.92
1975	2529	2432	1.04

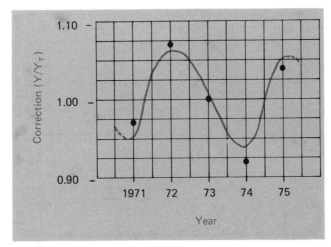

Figure 6–2. Cyclical correction factor.

Seasonal effects are present in many sales patterns, for industrial as well as for consumer products, and may have a large influence on monthly or quarterly sales and demand. A method for deriving correction factors is illustrated in (the partial) Table 6–6.

The complete table would, of course, have data for all twelve months of each of the years (preferably at least seven years). Beside each month's unit sales in this table is the fraction it represents of total sales for that year. For example, in January, 1960,

$$\frac{228}{3,625} = 0.063.$$

The January fractions are then averaged to give a seasonality correction factor for January, and the same is done for each of the remaining eleven months.

Table 6–6.

Month	1960 Sales (units)	1960 Monthly Fraction	1961 Sales (units)	1961 Monthly Fraction	1968 Monthly Fraction	Seasonality Correction Factor
Jan.	228	.063	224	.056	.061	.062
Feb.	213	.059	240	.060	.059	.062
Mar.	238	.066	272	.075	.069	.071
etc.						
Total Year	3,625	1.00	3,995	1.00	1.00	1.00

These fractions can then be applied to the sales forecast for, say, 1971 to get monthly forecasts, as in Table 6—7.

Table 6—7.

Year	Y_T	Month	Seasonality Correction Factor	Forecast Monthly Sales
1971	6,110	Jan.	0.062	379
		Feb.	0.062	379
		Mar.	0.071	434
		etc.		

If the data indicate that the seasonal pattern has shifted significantly with time, it may be desirable to use exponential smoothing[6] to put more emphasis on the data of recent years.

There are computer programs to decompose any series of sales or demand data into the long-term or secular trend, Y_T, the cyclical correction and the seasonality factor. When such is available, it should be preferred to these manual calculations because it would be quicker and more precise.

QUESTIONS AND EXERCISES

1   Choose a product for which you can obtain production or consumption data, by month, for at least nine years. Using simple regression against time, derive an expression in the form of Equation 6—1 or 6—4 for the secular trend. Then derive the cyclical and seasonal patterns, as in Section G. Finally, forecast for the next three years, by months.

2   Prepare the three-year forecast described in (1), above, deriving the secular trend by the econometric method of Section E.

3   For the specific product selected in (1) or (2), above, list the advantages and disadvantages of the naive vs. econometric method.

4   Choose a product (material, component, supply or equipment) or a service. Select a product aggregate, two direct derivative aggregates, and three end-product aggregates whose volumes might be appropriate as independent variables for econometric forecasting. State the advantages and disadvantages of using each of the aggregates for demand forecasting.

5   Why are leading indicators, such as housing starts, stock prices and the changes in money supply, seldom used in econometric forecasts of demand?

6   Prepare a three-year forecast (secular, only) for production of urea and melamine thermosetting plastics, based on the historical data plotted in Graph One in Appendix B, and using an appropriate naive method.

---

[6] Chisholm and Whitaker, *Forecasting Methods,* Irwin, 1974, pp. 22—26.

48

CHAPTER 7

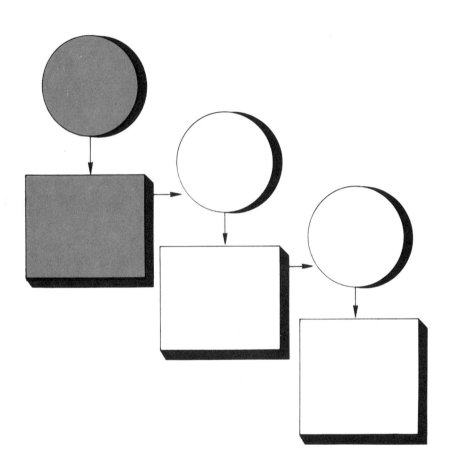

PRICE FORECASTING

A. The Hardest Forecast

Price forecasting is always difficult because prices do not follow simple engineering laws, or even ordinary accounting logic. They are usually the resultant of many forces, especially competition.

In a turbulent economy, price forecasting seems almost foolhardy; but it *must* be done, and it should be done with all the skill and science available.

B. Short-Range Price Forecasts

In forecasting prices up to perhaps two years into the future, there is no substitute for a detailed analysis of all cost elements and the probable effects of supply, demand and inflation. This analysis demands
- managerial accounting, with
- foresight and
- good judgment.

We start by examining all the elements of cost, from raw materials, services, labor and supervision; through packaging and shipping; all the way to advertising, sales overhead and administrative burden. For each element, we introduce our best estimate of the dollar effect of any shortages or over-supply, pay increase, anticipated import restriction and/or tariff, tax law or other change in government regulations.

We then look at demand for our product vs. supply, the aggressiveness of our competitors, and estimate the probability and the possible effects of

(1) a shortage that might support a price rise, or

(2) an attempt to buy market share by cutting price, regardless of the cost trend.

This process is intuitive, judgmental, subjective and an art. It is the best and only practical method for short-range price forecasting, especially in changing times.

C. Long-Range Price Forecasting

The managerial accounting approach is inadequate for long-range price forecasting — not because accounting fails, but because foresight fails. The key is productivity, five to ten or more years into the future.

Production people are unwilling to promise major cost savings from process or equipment improvements that have not yet been invented. Marketing researchers are unable to document expectations of major cost reductions. The results have been (1) price forecasts that proved to be far too optimistic, and (2) actual earnings considerably below estimates.

Therefore, we turn to an empirical method, called the experience curve method,[1] and use it with discretion. This method is related to the learning curve,[2] but takes into account all contributions to cost and price, not just labor and scale of operation.

---

[1] *Perspectives on Experience*, The Boston Consulting Group, 1972, pp. 12–22.

[2] Hirschman, "Profit from the Learning Curve," *Harvard Business Review*, Jan.–Feb. 1964, pp. 125–139. Kotler, *Marketing Decision Making: A Model Building Approach*, Holt, Rinehart and Winston, 1971, p. 230.

Experience Curve Method

The method is based on observations that the whole supply process becomes more efficient as

○ operators learn to do their jobs more rapidly,

○ aggressive producers improve their processes,

○ successful producers build bigger plants to reap the benefits of economy of scale, and

○ aggressive marketers become more efficient.

These four actions reduce the cost of production and marketing as experience accumulates.

Specifically, in efficient industries, unit costs expressed in constant dollars drop 20 to 30% each time cumulative volume doubles; and in a competitive business, prices also drop 20 to 30% each time cumulative volume doubles. This observation was shown by the Boston Consulting Group to be true for diodes, transistors, gas ranges, electric power, para-xylene, and even Japanese beer. Some Widener MBA students have found it applicable to fork lift trucks and home vacuum cleaners, as well.[3]

Those who are skeptical are in good company; for many industrial and academic people were skeptical, and a few still are. But the evidence seems overwhelming, *provided* we observe certain rules and use common sense in application.

Application of the Method

First, we express costs and prices in constant dollars, i.e., actual values divided by the GNP deflator. Second, we plot not against time, but against total volume accumulated from the beginning. When plotted on log-log paper, the points ordinarily indicate approximately straight lines. We can forecast by extrapolating the graphs, or analytically, as follows.

$$\frac{C_2}{C_1} = \left(\frac{V_2}{V_1}\right)^k \qquad \qquad \text{Equation 7-1}$$

$$\frac{P_2}{P_1} = \left(\frac{V_2}{V_1}\right)^k \qquad \qquad \text{Equation 7-2}$$

where

C_1 = cost at cumulative volume, V_1
P_1 = price at cumulative volume V_1
C_2 = cost at cumulative volume, V_2
P_2 = price at cumulative volume, V_2
k = a constant of negative sign.

In these equations, $k = -0.515$ if cost or price is dropping 30% for each doubling of cumulative volume. Having forecast in constant dollars, we multiply by the forecast GNP deflator to get cost or price in current dollars.

Notice that this requires us to forecast volume and the deflator before we can locate future cost or price in terms of time and express it in then-current dollars.

---

[3] Term papers by David E. Davis and James P. Spooner, submitted April, 1974, in partial satisfaction of requirements of Widener College's course in Forecasting and Corporate Planning.

Limitations on the Method

There are at least six influences that can distort this convenient relationship between price or cost and cumulative volume:

(1)   a shortage or glut of raw materials, producing a significant jump or drop in cost

(2)   an artificial change in cost and/or availability of raw materials resulting from government action

(3)   an artificial change in processing cost resulting from government action (e.g., on safety, on pollution abatement)

(4)   competitive moves that push profit margins up in a seller's market, or down in a recession

(5)   a patent that permits the holder to keep price up although cost is dropping with increasing experience

(6)   the effect of rapid inflation to enormously increase new plant cost.

When such a distortion is evident or expected, we must isolate that element of price and estimate its future contribution by judgment. The sum of the remaining elements (e.g., "value added", cost exclusive of raw materials) may be forecast by experience curve. Then we re-combine all elements and convert from constant to current dollars.

Ignoring these distortions can lead to quite unsatisfactory results, as was demonstrated by Stobaugh and Townsend[4] in an extensive series of regression analyses on prices of 82 petrochemicals.

Common Sense

Usually, the biggest stumbling-block to acceptance of this approach to price forecasting is our intuitive feeling that price cannot drop forever, that eventually it must level off and (we hope) rise. Indeed, this does happen when the product has matured and growth has slowed to such an extent that a long time is required to double cumulative volume. Then, the time rate of price decrease (fractional change in constant dollar price per year) becomes less than rate of inflation, and the combined effect is a price increase in current dollars (see Table 7—3 forecasts for 1975).

Examples

(1) Synthetic Staple and Tow: Table 7—1 summarizes the data that were used to draw the graph in Figure 7—1. It also includes forecasts for the four years, 1971—1974, calculated on the basis of facts that were available at the end of 1970. Annual production for 1971—1974 was assumed to continue the 20% per year average growth rate shown earlier, and the constant dollar prices for those years were calculated from the equation of the straight line in Figure 7—1. Factory prices were then calculated, using estimates of the GNP deflator to convert to current dollars.

The forecasts are compared with actual prices for 1971—1974 in Table 7—2. Through 1973, the forecasts are rather good, considering the fluctuating nature of the textile business and the fact that a capacity limitation developed in 1972 and/or

---

[4] Stobaugh and Townsend, "Price Forecasting and Strategic Planning: The Case of Petrochemicals", *Journal of Marketing Research,* Feb. 1975.

Table 7—1. Synthetic Staple and Tow*

		Data and Price Projection			
Year	Annual Production (millions of pounds)	Cumulative Production (millions of pounds)	Factory Price ($/lb)	GNP Deflator	Const. $ Price ($/lb)
1955	105	344	1.60	0.908	1.76
1960	240	1,296	1.26	1.032	1.22
1965	782	3,680	0.84	1,109	0.76
1970	1,797	10,861	0.41	1.353	0.30
1	2,100e	12,960e	0.41e	1.416e	0.29e
2	2,520e	15,480e	0.37e	1.461e	0.25e
3	3,020e	18,500e	0.34e	1.539e	0.22e
4	3,630e	22,130e	0.31e	1.638e	0.19e

*Excludes glass and cellulosic fibers.
Production figures, 1955 to 1970, from U.S. Dept. of Commerce, *1971 Business Statistics.*
Production estimates, 1971 to 1974, assume 20% growth/yr.
Prices are for polyester apparel staple, from Stanford Res. Inst.

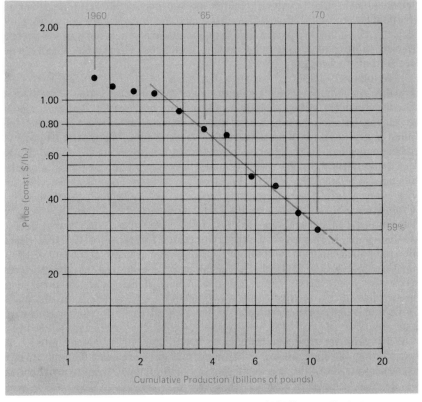

Production figures from U.S. Dept. of Commerce, *1971 Business Statistics.*
Prices for polyester apparel staple, from Stanford Research Institute.

Figure 7–1. Synthetic staple and tow, Price vs. cumulative production.

Table 7—2. Synthetic Staple and Tow.

	Actual vs. Forecast Prices					
	Price ($/lb.)		Production (millions of pounds)		GNP Deflator	
Year	Actual	Estimated	Actual	Estimated	Actual	Estimated
1971	0.38	0.41	2,105	2,100	1.416	1.416
1972	0.36	0.37	2,582	2,520	1.461	1.461
1973	0.38	0.34	2,970	3,020	1.531	1.539
1974	0.43	0.31	2,783	3,630	1.702	1.628

Actual prices for polyester apparel staple 1971—1973, from Stanford Research Institute, *Chemical Economics Handbook*, Oct. 1974. Figure for 1974 is industry estimate.
Actual production, 1971—1974, from U.S. Dept. of Commerce, *1973 Business Statistics*, and *Survey of Current Business*, 1973 to May, 1975.

1973. The rather abrupt price rise in 1974 probably is attributable to the jump in raw materials and energy costs triggered by the petroleum embargo of late 1973.

It should be noted that the production figures used in this example are for *all* synthetic staple and tow, because figures for polyester apparel staple alone were not available. This undoubtedly contributed to the unusually step slope in Figure 7—1 (prices dropping to 59% with each doubling of cumulative production); and it may have distorted the forecasts somewhat.

(2) Automobiles: Table 7—3 gives U.S. Department of Commerce data on domestic sales and indexed average prices from 1947 through 1970. These figures are shown graphically in Figure 7—2. Recalling the trends in the 1950s toward more powerful engines and power-operated brakes, steering, transmissions and windows, the lack of any steady price drop in those years seems to be explained. The product was being up-graded.

From about 1960 through 1970, however, the expected decrease with cumulative volume was observable, and the drop with doubling volume was about 32%.

Attention is drawn to the two estimates for 1975 in Table 7—3, which differ because of the GNP deflator estimates used. In the second of these, for which the deflator was taken as 1.82, the forecast price in current dollars shows a 10% increase over 1974. This is an example of the result of a more rapid rise in inflation than in the price benefit of experience.

(3) Gasoline: A case in which cost of the basic raw material fluctuated widely was described by Nathanson,[5] who subtracted this cost and applied the experience curve to value added, only. As shown in Figure 7—3, value added (expressed as 1958 constant cents per octane gallon) decreased rather uniformly at an average rate of about 36% for each doubling of cumulative production. Nathanson believed that in this capital-intensive business, construction costs probably account for the major inflationary effect, and he used a construction index as his deflator. He also reported that the data fitted a straight line (after about 1952) better when he used this index than when he used the GNP deflator.

---

[5] Nathanson, *Chemical Engineering Progress*, Nov. 1972, pp. 89—96.

Ref.: U.S. Dept. of Commerce, *1971 Business Statistics.*

Table 7—3. U.S. Automobiles (Factory domestic sales of new cars)

Year	Annual Sales (millions)	Cumulative Sales (millions)	Price Index (curr. $)	GNP Deflator	Price Index (const. $)
1947	3.3	63.3	69.2	0.746	93
1950	6.5	78.5	83.4	0.801	104
1953	5.9	93.7	95.8	0.883	108
1955	7.7	106.8	90.9	0.908	100
1958	4.1	122.5	101.5	1.000	102
1960	6.5	134.5	104.5	1.032	101
1962	6.8	146.7	104.1	1.057	99
1964	7.6	161.7	103.2	1.088	95
1966	8.3	179.1	99.1	1.130	87
1968	8.4	194.6	102.8	1.218	84
1970	6.2	208.6	107.6	1.353	80
1974	8e	241e	120e	1.628e	74e
1975*	8e	249e	118e	1.664e	72e
1975**	8e	249e	132e	1.82e	72e

*Calc'd assuming 2.2% inflation rate, 1975 vs 1974
**Calc'd assuming 12% inflation rate, 1975 vs 1974

Ref.: U.S. Dept. of Commerce, *1971 Business Statistics.*

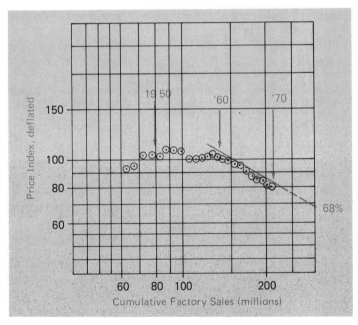

Ref.: U.S. Dept. of Commerce, *1971 Business Statistics.*

Figure 7—2. Automobiles (U.S., domestic, new)
Price vs. cumulative factory sales.

Price Forecasting

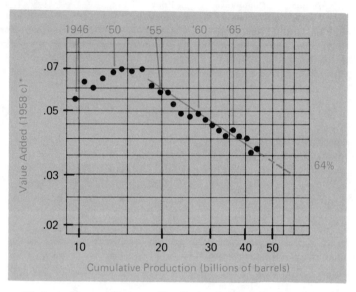

*Expressed as c per "octane gallon," using Construction Cost Index as
 deflator.
Ref: D.M. Nathanson, *Chem. Eng. Progress*, Nov. 1972, pp. 89–96.

Figure 7–3. Gasoline (U.S.) Value added vs. cumulative production.

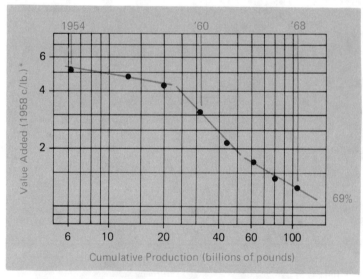

*Expressed as c/lb., using Construction Cost Index as deflator
Ref: D.M. Nathanson, *Chem. Eng. Progress*, Nov. 1972, pp. 89–96.

Figure 7–4. Ethylene (U.S.) Value added vs. cumulative production.

(4) Ethylene: Nathanson applied the experience curve to ethylene, again considering only value added and preferring a construction index as his deflator. He attributed the abrupt drop from about 1958 to 1963 (see Figure 7–4) to the effects of the change from prices dominated by coal-processing technology to prices dominated by petroleum-processing technology.

EXERCISES

1. Obtain historical data on price and annual consumption or production for a product, beginning with the earliest figures available[6]. Plot price against cumulative volume on log-log paper, and extrapolate the "best" line for use in forecasting. From the volume data, forecast cumulative volume for each of three future years. Read constant-dollar prices for these three years from the graph; and convert to current-dollar prices.
2. Make the same forecast as in (1) above; but assume that cost of a major raw material will follow some arbitrary pattern (such as a 5% annual rate of increase in constant dollars). Use the experience curve method to forecast price exclusive of that raw material. Forecast the cost of the raw material separately, and combine the two.

---

[6] To estimate the volume accumulated prior to your earliest data year, use the rule devised by the Boston Consulting Group: namely, "previous experience about equals the amount added in doubling the annual unit rate. Thus, if 5 years are required to double the annual rate, the sum of production in the 5 years approximates the cumulative experience at the beginning of the 5 years". *Perspectives on Experience.* Boston Consulting Group, 1972, p. 69.

CHAPTER 8

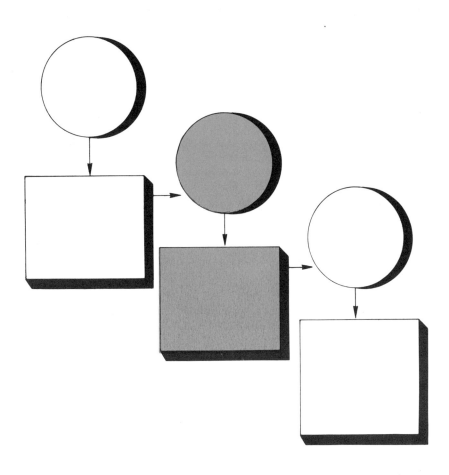

VALUE-IN-USE AND THE OPPORTUNITY CONCEPT

A. How Big Could the Market Be?

We have shown in Chapters 5 and 6, how demand for a product can be estimated. All but one of the methods assume that the product will continue to be used mostly as it has been in the past, and that any expansion or contraction in uses will continue to occur at the historical rate. The exception is the built-up sales forecast that includes the effects of some anticipated major shift in the requirements of a large customer or important market segment.

For consumer goods, such assumptions are almost universally acceptable. Consumers buy shoes to wear on their feet and are unlikely to buy them for use as door stops or book-ends. Similarly, they buy food to eat, not usually for home decoration. The end-uses are, therefore, easily defined.

For industrial goods, however, alternative uses are frequently possible. Expressed another way, industrial applications can be satisfied, in most cases, by more than one material, or by more than one design of component part. The specific material or component part that is preferred at any given time will normally be the one that is most economical to use, out of all that qualify technically.

This does not mean that the most economical product or component is always used. Tradition or inertia may discourage innovation. But managers want to know the size of the markets in which their products are

○ technically adequate and

○ economically competitive,

because these are their potential target markets. Given this information, they can direct campaigns to sell their products in these markets.

B. Value-in-Use

Setting aside, for the moment, the question of appraising technical adequacy, let us consider how to estimate the economic value of an alternative product. We want a method that is realistic, and a measure of value that is so persuasive that it can be used by salesmen as an argument to convince customers.

Ideally, the salesmen want to be able to say, in effect, "In your application, our product is worth X; and X is so much larger than Y, the price of our product, that the difference offers you a significant saving."

"Value-in-Use" is the calculated worth of an alternative (or "candidate") product when substituted for the product now in use (the "incumbent"). If Value-in-Use is greater than the price of the candidate, the candidate should be used. The greater the difference between Value-in-Use and price, the greater the incentive for a change to the candidate product.

To calculate Value-in-Use of a candidate material, we first calculate the cost of using the incumbent material. We call this its "Use Cost". This includes not only the price of that material in cents per pound (or gallon, or square yard, etc.), but also the cost of processing, the cost of any finishing operations, the scrap cost, the inventory charges associated with stocking the material, and any other significant item of cost.

Similarly, the Use Cost of an incumbent *component part* includes not only its purchase price, but also the costs of assembly, adjustment, etc.

Finally, if we are comparing two materials, or two components, whose useful lives differ, and if the difference is valuable, we should take this into account by calculating use cost per year, or "Annual Use Cost". Equation 8–1, below, would be used to calculate this for an incumbent material.

$$\text{Ann. Use Cost}_{(\text{inc.})} = (QC + C_p + C_f + \ldots) \div L \qquad \text{Equation } 8-1$$

where Q = quantity of incumbent material per unit quantity of finished product.

C = purchase price of incumbent material per unit quantity.

C_p = processing cost per unit quantity of finished product, using the incumbent material.

C_f = finishing cost per unit of finished product, using the incumbent material.

L = useful life of finished product, using the incumbent material.

A similar equation would be used to express the Annual Use Cost of the candidate material. However, in this equation, we insert, not the price of the candidate, but an unknown, V, which is the Value-in-Use of the candidate. We then equate the two Annual Use Costs and solve for V.[1]

To illustrate, take a simplified example. Let us assume that an industrial fastener is being produced of die-cast alloy, and our candidate material is a sheet metal from which the fastener could be fabricated by a combination punching-forming process. Suppose that the pertinent quantities and costs are those in Table 8–1.

Table 8–1. Industrial Fastener.

Cost Element	Die-Cast	Sheet Metal
Quantity per finished part, lb.	0.05	0.03
Price of material, $/lb.	0.25	0.20
Fabricating cost, $/part	0.05	0.10
Finishing cost, $/part	0.02	0
Inventory cost, %**	5	5
Scrap cost, %**	10	20
Useful life of finished parts, years	3	7

**Percentages are based on value of material in finished part.

---

[1] In some cases, Value-in-Use must be calculated from equations for contribution to profits, rather than from use costs.

First, we calculate the Annual Use Cost of the incumbent material, using Equation 8–2.

$$\text{Ann.Use Cost}_{(inc.)}=(QC+C_{fab;}+C_{fin.}+XQC+YQC)\div L \quad \text{Equation 8–2}$$

where   X   =   inventory cost, expressed as a decimal fraction
           Y   =   scrap cost, expressed as a decimel fraction,
Inserting the numbers from Table 6–1 and solving, we get:

$$
\begin{aligned}
\text{Ann.Use Cost}_{(inc.)} &= (QC + 0.05 + 0.02 + 0.05\,QC + 0.1\,QC) \div 3 \\
&= (1.15\,QC + 0.07) \div 3 \\
&= (1.15 \times 0.05 \times 0.25 + 0.07) \div 3 \\
&= (0.014375 + 0.07) \div 3 \\
&= 0.084375 \div 3 \\
&= 0.0281 \text{ (rounded)}
\end{aligned}
$$

Second, we set up a similar equation for the Annual Use Cost of the candidate material (Equation 8–3) and simplify it, as follows.

$$
\begin{aligned}
\text{Ann.Use Cost}_{(cand)} &= (Q'V+C'_{fab.} + X'Q'V+Y'Q'V) \div L' \quad \text{Equation 8–3} \\
&= (Q'V+0.10 + 0.05\,Q'V+0.2\,Q'V) \div 7 \\
&= (1.25\,Q'V+0.10) \div 7 \\
&= (1.25 \times 0.03\,V+0.10) \div 7 \\
&= (0.0375\,V+0.10) \div 7 \\
&= 0.00536\,V+0.0143
\end{aligned}
$$

Finally, we equate the two expressions for Annual Use Costs and solve for Value-in-Use of the candidate material:

$$
\begin{aligned}
0.00536\,V &+ 0.0143 = 0.0281 \\
0.00536\,V &= 0.0281 - 0.0143 = 0.0138 \\
V &= 0.0138 \div 0.00536 \\
V &= 2.57
\end{aligned}
$$

This tells us that if the sheet metal cost $2.57 per pound, its Annual Use Cost would just match that of the die-cast alloy. In other words, for this hypothetical application, the sheet metal is *worth* $2.57 per pound; that is, its Value-in-Use is $2.57 per pound. This is so much greater than its assumed price of $0.20 per pound, that the fabricator would be wise to adopt the sheet metal.

We could of course, have simply put the price of the sheet metal into Equation 8–3, rather than the unknown, V. In this case, we would have found the Annual Use Cost of the sheet metal fastener to be $0.00154 per year. Comparison with the Annual Use Cost of the die-cast fastener, $0.0281 per year, shows the candidate would cost only 55% as much as the incumbent, and that the fabricator would save $0.0127 in Annual Use Cost per part made.[2] It is more impressive, however, to

---

[2] This might be confusing to our customer because of the different useful lives of the two fasteners.

compare the Value-in-Use of the candidate with its price, and to show the saving of $2.37 for each pound of sheet metal used. Either way, the sheet metal salesman would have a persuasive argument in favor of his product.

C. Functional Potential

Now, let us look at the matter of technical adequacy of a material or a component part for a potential application.

We need to ascertain as closely as possible the real technical requirements of the application. These are not necessarily the properties of the material or component now being used, for the incumbent may be over-qualified for the application. In some cases, it may be under-qualified and be the source of some dissatisfaction on the part of the customer or the end-users.

To get a first approximation of the technical requirements, we may look at the properties of the incumbent, and these may be readily available in published manuals or in the sales literature of the suppliers. For a material, they may comprise (1) physical properties, such as density, tensile strength, abrasion resistance, and service temperature, and (2) processing properties, such as molding cycle time for a plastic, casting temperature for an alloy, and curing time for a paint. For a component part, they may comprise such characteristics as horse-power rating for a motor, maximum and minimum service temperatures for an instrument, output signal current limits for a process transmitter, PV limit for a bearing, etc.

There is, however, no good substitute for knowledge of the *true* technical requirements, and this knowledge probably will be obtainable (if at all) only from a customer's or an end-user's design engineer. Time and patient, persistent questioning may be required to get the best available estimates. Often even the designer does not know the precise requirements.

We must assemble a set of technical requirements for each application to be considered. These applications should be not only the current applications (if any) for our candidate, but also as many untried applications as we may think have even a remote chance of presenting suitable markets. The task is tedious, but it can be very rewarding.

The next step is to assemble the physical properties, processing or fabricating characteristics, and performance characteristics of the candidate. There may be fifty or more data involved; and although only four or five may be critical for any one application, a different set may be critical for the next application.

Having a data bank of technical requirements for all the applications and another data bank of properties of our candidate, we then methodically compare properties with requirements to find all the applications for which the candidate appears to be technically adequate, and to reject those for which it would not.

Finally, for each of the applications our candidate would seem to satisfy, we need to estimate current and future demand, in terms of the quantity of our candidate required. The sum of these demands is called Functional Potential, and it is always expressed as a quantity (units, pounds, gallons, etc.) per unit of time at a specified point in time; e.g., 5,000,000 lbs. per year in 1985.

D. Opportunity

Functional Potential, while useful, is impractical because it probably includes "demand" for applications in which our candidate would not be economically competitive with the incumbent materials or component parts.

Therefore, we collect prices, processing or assembly costs, finishing costs, etc., and calculate Value-in-Use (see above) for each application included in our estimate of Functional Potential. We reject those applications for which our candidate's Value-in-Use is less than its price, and add the demands of the remaining applications. The sum is called Opportunity,[3] (or, sometimes, Functional Potential, Cost-Considered), and it is expressed as a quantity per unit of time at a specified point in time, e.g., 3,100,000 lbs. per year in 1985.

Note that, to be useful, our calculation must take into account expected future changes in prices and costs. If our candidate is a new product whose price may be expected to decrease with time (because of improvements in process or the economies of scale) more rapidly than the price of older incumbents, we may conclude that certain applications now excluded should later become a part of our future Opportunity.

A rigorous exclusion from Opportunity of each application in which our candidate's Value-in-Use is not exactly equal to its price may not be realistic, either. This is true because some customers and end-users have a rather broad range of discrimination. A saving of a half-cent per pound, or per unit, may not be enough to justify changing from the incumbent to our candidate. Perhaps the change would complicate a customer's inventory system, or require installation of new processing equipment and re-training his operators. Perhaps inertia or a preference for his traditional way of operating makes him reluctant to change. Perhaps the end-user believes his advertising claim that he uses only certain well-known materials or components gives him a competitive edge. This gives the marketing researcher a choice: (1) he may take the conservative position of setting appropriate margins above the candidate's price, deciding that only this higher Value-in-Use will be acceptable in selecting the applications to be included in his estimate of Opportunity, or (2) he may be optimistic that time and good salesmanship might ultimately overcome the obstacles. Accordingly, he should be sure to tell his marketing people which choice he has made.

E. The Validity of Opportunity

Opportunity is not a demand forecast. The candidate may never be used in all of the applications that theoretically would be satisfied. It is demand at the saturation point, a long-range, utopian goal that probably will never be reached, for both practical and emotional reasons.

Note also that Opportunity applies equally to all generically equivalent candidates (e.g., to all acetic acid, to all truly interchangeable electric motors, to all

---

[3] Ref: Gee, Robert E., "The Opportunity Criterion — A New Approach to the Evaluation of R & D", *Research Management,* May, 1972, pp. 64-71.
Borcherdt, Gerald T., "Design of the Marketing Program for a New Product", in Clewett (ed.), *Marketing's Role in Scientific Management,* American Marketing Association, 1957, pp. 58-73.

substantially identical zinc die-casting alloys). We shall consider the matter of market share in Chapter 9.

Nevertheless, Opportunity can be extremely useful in guiding marketing people.[4] It can help end-use development specialists and salesmen by pointing out the largest of the untapped markets, and it can show which of these are most likely to be realized as the result of the incentive provided by high Value-in-Use/price ratios.

It can also point out current applications that may be threatened by competitive products, if the marketing researcher has estimated Opportunity for his leading competitors' products as well as for his company's product. If a significant number of the applications considered in his Opportunity estimate are thus jeopardized, he may discover that his company's current sales actually exceed his calculated Opportunity. Naturally, he should call his marketing people's attention to this fact, pointing out which competitive products may replace his company's product, and what improvements in product characteristics or decrease in price would be necessary to counter the threats. (See the section on Simulations, Chapter 9).

F. An Example[5]

We shall assume that a new plastic molding resin, especially formulated to provide a low coefficient of friction, is to be offered for the molding of small industrial bearings. Additional expected advantages over many bearing materials are

1. Higher PV limit
2. Lower wear factor (rate)
3. Higher maximum service temperature
4. Longer maintenance-free operation.

Among the many possible applications, we shall consider only the following seven, for simplicity.

Application	Assumed Principal Incumbent
Fractional horsepower motors	bronze
Small appliances	acetal resin
Door hinges	acetal resin
Business machines	fluorocarbon resin
Optical devices	polycarbonate resin
Lawn mowers	nylon resin
Audio components	nylon resin

The assumed technical requirements of these applications are shown in Table 8–2.

If our new resin, to which we shall give the fictitious name "M-R-ite", were used in all these applications, the demands estimated for each of three years would be those given in Table 8–3. We call these demands "multipliers".

Comparing properties of M-R-ite with technical requirements of the applications

---

[4] An analogous approach for consumer goods is described in John A. Weber, *Growth Opportunity Analysis*, Reston, 1976.

[5] Adapted from a term paper by Joseph Cuneo, submitted April 29, 1975, in partial satisfaction of requirements of Widener College's graduate course in Marketing Research.

in Table 8—2, we easily see that M-R-ite should be technically adequate for all except

1. fractional horsepower motors, for which it shows insufficient tensile strength, insufficient PV, excessive coefficient of friction, and excessive wear,
2. optical devices, in which it could not provide transparency.

Functional Potentials for M-R-ite in the three years are obtained by summing the multipliers for the remaining five applications (see Table 8—5).

Table 8—2. Industrial Bearings.

			Requirements and Candidate Properties			
Technical Requirements of Applications						
Application	Minimum PV Limit	Minimum Tensile Strength	Maximum Wear Factor	Maximum Coefficient of Friction	Min.Upper Service Temperature	Other
Fractional HP Motors	10,000	15,000	5	0.11	120	—
Small Appliances	2,500	9,000	100	0.28	150	—
Door Hinges	100	7,500	50	0.45	120	—
Business Machines	100	2,000	75	0.19	200	—
Optical Devices	50	1,500	25	0.22	180	Must be transparent
Lawn Mowers	1,900	10,000	15	0.30	120	—
Audio Components	200	5,000	10	0.22	150	—
Properties of Candidate						
M-R-ite	4,000	13,700	7	0.15	220	Opaque

Before proceeding to estimates of Opportunity, we must calculate Value-in-Use for each of the five applications and compare it with our assumed price of 4.3 cents/in.^{3} (approximately $0.78/lb.) for M-R-ite. For simplicity, we shall assume constant prices of all materials during the three years under consideration. Hypothetical values for quantities of resin needed per bearing, prices of incumbent materials, costs of fabricating and finishing, and useful lives of the bearings are given in Table 8—4.

Estimates of Value-in-Use would be made as follows.

(1) Small Appliances

Ann. Use Cost$_{(inc.)}$ = (QP + C$_{fab.}$ + C$_{fin.}$) ÷ L

Ann. Use Cost$_{(cand.)}$ = (Q'V + C'$_{fab.}$ + C'$_{fin.}$) ÷ L'

Note that expected life of appliances is assumed to be 10 years, making L = L' = 10.

(QP + C$_{fab.}$ + C$_{fin.}$) ÷ L=(Q'V + C'$_{fab.}$ + C'$_{fin.}$) ÷ L'

(0.05 × 3.1 + 2 + 0) ÷ 10 = (0.05 V + 3 + 0) ÷ 10

2.155 ÷ 10 = (0.05 V + 3) ÷ 10

2.155 = 0.05 V + 3

0.05 V = 2.155 − 3 = −0.845

V = −16.9c/in.^{3}

M-R-ite is clearly not economically competitive in this application, and the multipliers for small appliances are not to be included in Opportunity.

Table 8–3. Industrial Bearings.

Application	Multipliers (Estimated Demands)					
	Multipliers in Year 1		Multipliers in Year 2		Multipliers in Year 3	
	Volume (mil. in.^{3})	Weight of M-R-ite* (1000 lbs.)	Volume (mil. in.^{3})	Weight of M-R-ite* (1000 lbs.)	Volume (mil. in.^{3})	Weight of M-R-ite* (1000 lbs.)
Fractional HP Motors	125	6,875	143	7,865	157	8,635
Small Appliances	242	13,310	267	14,685	280	15,400
Door Hinges	5	275	7	385	8	440
Business Machines	38	2,090	51	2,805	63	3,465
Optical Devices	12	660	16	880	22	1,210
Lawn Mowers	17	935	20	1,100	32	1,760
Audio Components	84	4,620	104	5,720	139	7,645
Totals		28,765		33,440		38,555

*Assuming density of M-R-ite is 0.055 lb./in.^{3}

Table 8–4. Industrial Bearings.

Data for Value-in-Use Calculations

	Quantity of Resin (in.³/ bearing)	Incumbent Material				Candidate Material		
		Price (c/in.³)	Fabrication (c/bearing)	Finishing (c/bearing)	Life (Yrs.)	Fabrication (c/bearing)	Finishing (c/bearing)	Life (Yrs.)
Fractional HP Motors	0.1	18.0	9	3	15	4	1	40
Small Appliances	0.05	3.1	2	0	30*	3	0	40*
Door Hinges	0.005	3.1	1	0	20	2	0	40
Business Machines	0.02	23.3	1.5	0	10	3	0	40
Optical Devices	0.03	3.6	3	2	5	3	1	40
Lawn Mowers	0.1	3.3	3	0	5**	3	0	10**
Audio Components	0.06	3.3	3	0	8	3	0	40

*Assume average expected life of appliances is 10 years.
**Assume average expected life of lawn mowers is 2 years.

(2) Door Hinges

Ann. Use $\text{Cost}_{(inc.)} = (0.005 \times 3.1 + 1 + 0) \div 20$

Ann. Use $\text{Cost}_{(cand.)} = (0.005\ V + 2 + 0) \div 40$

$1.0155 \div 20 = (0.005\ V + 2) \div 40$

$0.050775 = 0.000125\ V + 0.05$

$V = 6.20c/\text{in.}^3$

> V is, therefore, greater than the assumed price of the candidate, 4.3 cents per cubic inch, and the multipliers for door hinges should be included in Opportunity.

(3) Business Machines

Ann. Use $\text{Cost}_{(inc.)} = (0.02 \times 23.3 + 1.5 + 0) \div 10$

Ann. Use $\text{Cost}_{(cand.)} = (0.02\ V + 3 + 0) \div 40$

$(0.02 \times 23.3 + 1.5) \div 10 = (0.02\ V + 3) \div 40$

$0.1966 = 0.0005\ V + 0.075$

$V = 243.2$

> The multipliers for business machines should be included in Opportunity.

(4) Lawn Mowers

Ann. Use $\text{Cost}_{(inc.)} = (0.1 \times 3.3 + 3 + 0) \div 2$

Ann. Use $\text{Cost}_{(cand.)} = (0.1\ V + 3 + 0) \div 2$

> By inspection of these expressions, it is seen $V = 3.3$, so the multipliers should not be included in Opportunity.

(5) Audio Components

Ann. Use $\text{Cost}_{(inc.)} = (0.06 \times 3.3 + 3 + 0) \div 8$

Ann. Use $\text{Cost}_{(cand.)} = (0.06\ V + 3 + 0) \div 40$

$0.39975 = 0.0015\ V + 0.075$

$V = 216.5$

> The multipliers should be included in Opportunity.

With these estimates of Value-in-Use, we are now ready to assemble the multipliers, as in Table 8–5, showing both Functional Potential and Opportunity.

Our final step is to prepare a graph of the results, for clarity in presenting the results to marketing managers, as shown in Figure 8–1.

EXERCISES

1. Calculate Functional Potential and Opportunity for a fictional blue pigment dispersion having the properties shown in Table 8–6, given the technical requirements in Table 8–7 and the multiplier data in Table 8–8. In this exercise, make the economic comparison on the basis of price, in the absence of any use cost factors.

Table 8—5. Industrial Bearings

Application	Functional Potential and Opportunity		
	Year 1 (1000 lbs.)	Year 2 (1000 lbs.)	Year 3 (1000 lbs.)
Functional Potentials			
Small Appliances	13,310	14,685	15,400
Door Hinges	275	385	440
Business Machines	2,090	2,805	3,465
Lawn Mowers	935	1,100	1,760
Audio Components	4,620	5,720	7,645
Total Functional Potential	21,230	24,695	28,710
Opportunities			
Door Hinges	275	385	440
Business Machines	2,090	2,805	3,465
Audio Components	4,620	5,720	7,645
Total Opportunity	6,985	8,910	11,550

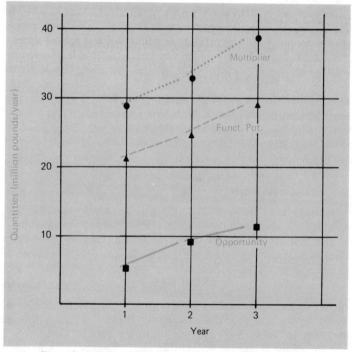

Figure 8—1. Industrial bearings. Total multiplier, functional potential and opportunity for M-R-ite.

Table 8—6. Blue Pigment Dispersion.

Characteristics of Candidate	
Color Co-ordinates	x=25, y=15, a=2.3
Strength	3 X 10⁻⁴ in oil
	1.2 X 10⁻⁴ in water
Dispersion	14
UV Stability	95 days
Form	75% ground in mineral spirits
	65% ground in water
Price	$2.45/lb. pigment content.

2. Calculate Value-in-Use, Multiplier, Functional Potential and Opportunity for an oriented, extruded strip of polypropylene that might replace ordinary metal hinges, given the technical requirements in Table 8—9, the multiplier data in Table 8—10, and the use cost factors in Table 8—11. Assume the polypropylene strip hinge used in each application would be as long as the box (e.g., 72" in the case of freezers and funeral caskets), and that the price of the polypropylene strip would be $0.12 per foot in Year 1, $0.10 per foot in Year 2, and $0.07 per foot in Year 3. Draw a graph showing Multiplier, Functional potential and Opportunity in millions of feet against time.

3. Select a candidate product for which you can consider at least seven actual or potential applications, and identify at least ten important physical properties. Obtain (or estimate) the four or five vital technical requirements of the seven applications, and the pertinent use cost factors for each application with the incumbent and with the candidate. Ascertain (or estimate) the expected useful life of both candidate and incumbent in each application, and calculate Value-in-Use. Calculate Multipliers, Functional Potential and Opportunity for each of three years, and plot against time.

Table 8–7. *Blue Pigment Dispersion.*

		Technical Requirements of Applications			
Requirement	Letterpress Ink	Rotogravure Ink	Latex Paint	Oil Base Paint	Plastics
Color co-ord.	x > 22	x > 24	x > 20	x > 20	x > 22
	y < 17	y < 14	y < 20	y < 20	y < 17
Strength, min.	a > 2.1	a < 2.0	a > 1.9	a > 2.2	a > 2.1
Dispersion, max.	2.9 in oil	2.5 in oil	1.0 in water	2.7 in oil	2.2 in oil
	15	15	20	.25	14
UV Stability, min.	—	—	10 days	50 days	50 days
Dispersable in	oil	oil	water	oil	alcohol
Max. Price, $/lb.	2.50	2.75	2.00	3.25	4.0

Table 8–8. *Blue Pigment Dispersion.*

	Data for Calculation of Multipliers				
	Quantities of Finished Product, mil. ann. lbs.				
Year	Letterpress Ink	Rotogravure Ink	Latex Paint	Oil Base Paint	Plastics
1	22.5	47.3	120	65	14
2	25.0	50.0	150	70	19
3	31.0	57.0	200	50	29
Characteristic			Factors, %		
Portion that is blue	15	15	17	12	3.5
Pigment content	70	70	50	45	2.1

Table 8—9. Polypropylene Hinge.

Property	Technical Requirements of Applications and Physical Properties of PP Hinge				
	Luggage, Tool & Tackle Boxes	Picnic Boxes & Ice Chests	Freezers and Funeral Caskets	Mobile Homes	Poly-propylene Strip
Min. no. flexures	5,000	500	750	7,000	10,000
Min. strength, lb./ft.	10	5	55	20	21
Min. weatherability, hrs.	1,000	500	—	—	1,500
Colorability?	Yes	—	Yes	Yes	Yes

Table 8—10. Polypropylene Hinge.

Year Incumbent Hinges	Multiplier Data			
	Luggage, Tool and Tackle Boxes	Picnic Boxes and Ice Chests	Freezers and Funeral Caskets	Mobile Homes
1 Number, mil./yr	10.0	1.2	2.2	1.0
Length, inches	24	16	72	36
Av. price, $/hinge	0.25	0.18	0.90	0.50
2 Number, mil./yr.	13.5	1.0	2.5	1.5
Length, inches	22	16	72	38
Av. price, $/hinge	0.24	0.17	0.85	0.50
3 Number, mil./yr.	15.2	0.8	3.0	1.8
Length, inches	20	15	72	40
Av. price, $/hinge	0.20	0.13	0.78	0.50

Table 8–11. Polypropylene Hinge.

| Year and Application* | Use Cost Factors | | | | | | |
| | Metal Hinge | | | Polypropylene Hinge | | | |
	Assembly ($ per hinge)	Inventory (% of hinge cost)	Spoilage (% of hinges)	Assembly ($ per hinge)	Inventory (% of hinge cost)	Spoilage (% of hinges)	Cutting Cost ($ per hinge)
1 Luggage, Tool & Tackle Boxes	0.03	10	3	0.05	5	7	0.01
Picnic Boxes & Ice Chests	0.05	10	2	0.05	5	5	0.01
Mobile Homes	0.05	10	3	0.06	4	5	0.01
2 Luggage, Tool & Tackle Boxes	0.04	10	6	0.04	5	6	0.005
Picnic Boxes & Ice Chests	0.05	10	2	0.04	5	5	0.005
Mobile Homes	0.05	10	3	0.04	4	4	0.007
3 Luggage, Tool & Tackle Boxes	0.04	10	4	0.03	5	5	0.005
Picnic Boxes & Ice Chests	0.05	10	2	0.03	5	4	0.005
Mobile Homes	0.05	10	2	0.03	4	3	0.005

*Factors not shown for freezers and caskets because polypropylene lacks strength required.

CHAPTER 9

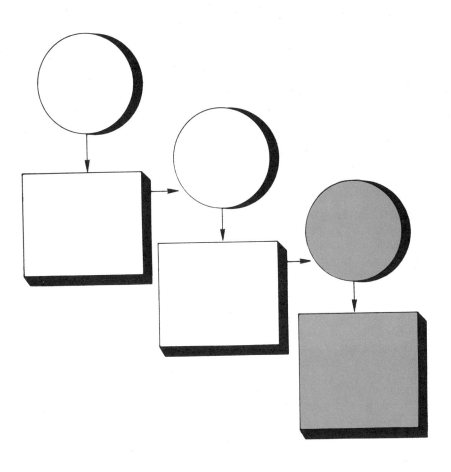

INFORMATION SYSTEMS, MODELS AND SIMULATION

A. The Computer's Contribution to Marketing

As has been observed in science, accounting and many other activities, the major contribution of the computer to marketing has not been simply to shorten the time and reduce the effort required to make the calculations that were being done "by hand". Instead, it has been to make affordable many tabulations and calculations that previously were abandoned or not attempted because the cost would have been excessive.

The computer seldom facilitates the collection of data. It can, however, assemble, analyze, compare, evaluate, aggregate, summarize and tabulate data to make them more easily understood. It can emphasize similarities, point out discrepancies, show relationships and make projections into the future. Finally, it can make judgments, providing that some human mind has given it criteria and rules to follow.

Thus, the computer is a labor-saving tool of marketing researchers and a boon to marketing managers who invariably wish for more and better information on

○ the markets they seek and serve, and
○ the effects of their marketing efforts.

B. Marketing Information Systems

Every marketing organization has some kind of a marketing information system. It may be very simple or very complete and complex. It may be no more than the minimum accounting records, plus the marketing manager's memory of his customers' activities and needs, and his awareness of the moves being made by his competitors.

On the other extreme, it may be an exhaustive compilation of many details coupled with capability to analyze, compare, rearrange, forecast, and summarize almost any imaginable combination of sales data, market shares, economic trends and so on.

We shall not attempt to describe any specific marketing information system, because much has already been published[1], and because every system should be tailored to the needs of the firm that will use it. However, we shall describe how a typical system grows in the absence of planning, and we shall list some of the prerequisites to designing an effective marketing information system.

The original marketing information system in the average firm was a tabulation of sales data, including details of product type, package size and style, quantity sold, customer's name and address, dates of order and shipment, etc. As the needs

---

[1] Buzzell, Cox and Brown, *Marketing Research and Information Systems*, McGraw-Hill, 1969, pp. 3—66, 695—779.
Clark and Sexton, *Marketing and Management Science: A Synergism*, Irwin, 1970, pp. 1—59.
Cox and Enis, *The Marketing Research Process*, Goodyear, 1972, pp. 511—545.
Giragosian (ed.), *Chemical Marketing Research*, Reinhold, 1967, pp. 305—310.
Montgomery and Urban, *Management Science in Marketing*, Prentice-Hall, 1969, pp. 17—26.
Simon and Freimer, *Analytical Marketing*, Harcourt, Brace and World, 1970, pp. 277—290.
Schoner and Uhl, *Marketing Research: Information Systems and Decision Making*, 2nd ed. Wiley, 1975, pp. 19—43.

arose, other details were added, such as the nature of the customer's business or process, the products he made, the end-uses and end-users of those products. Perhaps details of distribution were included, such as the warehouse or factory from which the shipment was made, the carrier used, the freight and delivery costs, and so on. If properly recorded, arranged and analyzed, these data could be sorted and aggregated to show total sales in any time period by type of customer, by sales territory, by shipment quantity, by package, by end-use, etc.

Further elaboration made it possible to compare sales in any category during a recent month or year with those of some earlier period, and to calculate rate of sales growth or decline. When sales objectives were incorporated, comparisons of actual sales versus objectives became possible.

Such elaboration soon made the complete record so bulky that reading the entire report, or even searching for a few critical items became too time-consuming for the busy marketing manager. To help him, the sales analysis staff prepared exception reports giving only unusually high or low sales (relative to sales objectives or to historical patterns), so that he would see only the items that indicated trouble or unexpected success. He also asked for special reports, concentrating on a few markets, products or customers. Sometimes these were prepared regularly. Often they were prepared only to illuminate the details behind the exceptions.

When this marketing information system was converted into computerized data banks and analysis programs, the drudgery was reduced and the reports generally became available sooner. This was especially true when the marketing manager was provided with a terminal in his office and taught how to access the system for any specific segments he needed to see. If he was an enthusiastic information seeker, he almost invariably showered his sales analysts with requests to include more data and programs to provide new arrays and aggregates.

Success was not frequently achieved smoothly, however. Beyond the usual debugging troubles, most marketing information systems proved to be much less than satisfactory because they failed to anticipate the volume of data and the proliferation of analyses that soon were desired by marketing managers. The managers usually had not spent enough time visualizing their needs, and the systems analysts knew too little about marketing to ask the right questions, at the time the system was being designed.

Both marketing people and systems analysts, in a firm embarking on a marketing information system of sufficient magnitude and complexity to justify the use of a computer, should carefully read the advice of earlier users[2].

This is where the marketing researcher can be extremely helpful. He should not be burdened with the operation of the system, but he definitely should be responsibly involved in its design and in any subsequent modifications. He knows from his intimate acquaintance with the marketing process what data can be incorporated into the data banks and what output may be most important. He also knows rather well what kinds of questions the marketing manager may ask, for he has been answering such questions in the past. He is particularly sensitive to those questions he was not able to answer because the data were not collected, or perhaps details had been lost by aggregation.

---

[2] E. g., Clark and Sexton (op. cit.), Chapters 1–3, pp. 1–59.

In the design stage, the marketing researcher will, naturally, seek to incorporate the capacity to collect, store, analyze and retrieve some information that he expects to use in offering new and expanded marketing research services to the marketing manager. This is his golden opportunity. If he does not grasp it, he may not only find it necessary to work with, or around, a system that ignores his needs, but he may also find the marketing information system encroaching on his functions so that he is left with fewer opportunities to make a significant contribution to marketing strategy. As Farley put it, "Generally speaking, researchers can either participate actively in the computerizing and model building activities involved in system development, or else they will find themselves increasingly isolated from the firm's data management activities and find their activities more and more circumscribed by other segments of the system design and development task forces."[3]

To recapitulate, in designing a marketing information system, great care must be taken to understand the range of decisions that must be made by all of its users, to define the specific information they require (and may require in the foreseeable future) in order to make those decisions, and to ascertain the input data that can be made available within practical limits. The users will be marketing management, field sales personnel, marketing researchers, and probably top management. Their specific needs will vary as to content, degree of aggregation, and frequency of reporting. Provision should be made for expansion of data banks, addition of programs to manipulate the data, and new displays. All of this takes time, patience and open communication between all parties concerned.

The system probably will be designed to include

(1)   Banks of in-company data on sales, sales objectives, customers, potential customers, end-users, distribution, sales force activities, shipments, returns, complaints, costs, revenues and some measure of profits — all in considerable detail.

(2)   Banks of external data on measurements of economic activity (economic indicators), industry-wide consumption, market trends, etc. — both historical and forecast,

(3)   Processing capabilities to compare current sales with objectives and with past sales, to calculate running averages, to calculate growth rates, to forecast future sales by regression against time (with or without cyclical and seasonal corrections, and exponential smoothing, if applicable), to forecast future sales by regression against economic indicators (econometric method), to estimate current and future market share, and perhaps to make similar comparisons and forecasts for sales force requirements, costs, revenues and earnings,

(4)   Processing capability for file transformation, file reorganization, file updating, and perhaps for simulation,

(5)   Print-out and display capability, with wide flexibility.

C. Models for Marketing Research

Every marketing manager has in his mind some picture of the effects that his

---

[3] John U. Farley, "Information Systems, Buyer Behavior and Industrial Marketing Research", Chemical Marketing Research Assn. Paper No. 682, New York Meeting, Apr. 29—May 1, 1970.

marketing efforts probably have on his sales volume and profits. Likewise, he has some visualization of the effects of economic trends, of government regulations and of the activities of his competitors. His "picture" may be more sub-conscious than conscious, it may be largely qualitative, and it may be based on relations that he could not describe exactly, even in words. However, it is the basis on which he decides whether to increase or decrease his advertising efforts, to add or subtract from his sales force, to raise or lower his price, to provide more or less technical service, and so on. It is his model of the marketplace, although he may not use that term to describe it.

All but the most intuitive marketing managers probably would admit that they could make more effective decisions if they had quantitative expressions of these relations.

Quantitative relations, or models, have been used quite effectively and for many years in production, in inventory managing and in engineering where the relations between actions and result are measurable and reproducible. Marketing, however, involves many actions that are difficult to measure with any precision, because they deal with human judgment. For example, an improvement in the design of a machine housing may seem highly desirable to the designer but inconsequential to many users. Likewise, the real value of more technical service may seem high to some purchasers, neutral to others and useless to still others.

Furthermore, the variables of a marketing strategy are usually highly interrelated. More advertising may or may not be affective, depending on product characteristics, distribution efficiency and/or salesmen's proficiencies. In other words, the variables often are not really independent, and their separate effects may not be measurable without considerable ambiguity.

Nevertheless, considerable effort has been expended in developing models to describe various aspects of marketing[4]. Most of this effots has been applied to the marketing of consumer goods, and some of the concepts are adaptable to industrial marketing. We shall mention several of these, and describe a few in some detail.

D. Forecasting Models

The equations developed in Chapter 6 (e.g., Equations 6–2, 6–5, 6–7 and 6–8) are models, although we did not use the term there. Each of them describes an apparent effect of the marketing environment on demand. The independent variable was time, alone, in the naive forecasts, whereas several independent variables (economic indicators) appeared in the econometric forecasting models. As stated in that chapter, the calculations to establish and use time series models are rather simple, but multiple regressions against several economic indicators are tedious without a computer.

In the same sense, Equation 7–2 is a price forecasting model, because it

---

[4] Amstutz, *Consumer Simulation of Competitive Market Response*, M.I.T. Press, 1967.
Clark and Sexton, *Marketing and Management Science: A Synergism*, Irwin, 1970.
King, *Quantitative Analysis for Marketing Management*, McGraw-Hill, 1967.
Kotler, *Marketing Decision Making: A Model Building Approach*, Holt, Rinehart & Winston, 1971.
Montgomery and Urban, *Management Science in Marketing*, Prentice-Hall, 1969.
Simon and Freimer, *Analytical Marketing*, Harcourt, Brace and World, 1970.

describes the apparent relation of price to the "independent" variable, cumulative volume (or, more correctly, to time and/or the economic indicators that enable us to forecast cumulative volume).

Several much more sophisticated models have been constructed by Arthur D. Little, Inc. to forecast both demand and price for the fertilizer industry[5] and for segments of the plastics industry[6]. In these, the effects of capacity limitations, production costs, inventory control, non-generic competition and profitability are included. The models also incorporate decision rules to predict new plant construction and its effects on capacity utilization, market shares and price. Feedback from one segment of the models to another enables them to simulate the effects of price on demand, of capacity utilization on costs and profitability, etc.

Hegeman reports that one of A. D. Little's models has been used continuously for several years by a plastics manufacturer. At least three other very similar models, developed independently by industrial marketing researchers, are known to have been in use since before 1971.

A summary article by Giragosian[7] lists and describes (mostly in general terms) several models developed by consulting and industrial firms for forecasting and simulation. Consulting firms included are Chase Econometric Associates, Inc., Data Resources, Inc., Econoscope (General Electric Co.), and Merrill Lynch Economics. User companies mentioned are Atlantic Richfield Co., Exxon Chemical Co., FMC Corp., W. R. Grace & Co., Shell Chemical Co., and Velsicol Chemical Corp. In one example, by Merrill Lynch & Co., Inc., of a model for a new pharmaceutical product, several variables are listed and mathematical equations for their effects on demand are given.

Whitfield[8] described a petrochemical model, constructed by Data Resources, Inc., to forecast prices and volumes from factors including the general economy, government regulation of the industry, price and availability of feedstocks, technological developments and the prices of substitutes. A typical demand equation in the model is

$$\text{Quantity of Low Density Polyethylene} = 6.45$$
$$-0.29 \ (\text{Price of Low Density Polyethylene})$$
$$+0.46 \ (\text{Index of End Market Activity}).$$

E. Models for Controllable Marketing Variables

Early models developed for consumer goods considered the effects on sales or market share of one controllable variable at a time, such as price, advertising, personal selling, promotion, and distribution. Many of these are not applicable to industrial goods: for example, although a retailer can cut price unilaterally for a special sale, or even for an extended period, the supplier of industrial products will

---

[5] Giragosian, *Chemical Marketing Research,* Reinhold, 1967, pp. 320–329.
[6] Hegeman, *The Art of Price Forecasting,* A. D. Little, Inc., pp. 8–12.
[7] Giragosian, "Econometric Models", Chemical Marketing Research Assn., Paper No. 999, Virginia Beach Meeting, Sept., 1976.
[8] Whitfield, "Forecasting Techniques via Econometric Models," Chemical Marketing Research Assn., Paper No. 967, New York Meeting, May, 1976.

find that the news of a price cut travels rapidly from one purchasing agent to the others. If he has any effective competition-in-kind, his price cut will be matched (perhaps retroactively) so soon as to vitiate any sales advantage he thought to achieve.

Similarly, brand-switching models are scarcely applicable to industrial marketing where a large customer may be loyal to two or more suppliers simultaneously, dividing his purchases to assure supply in case of a strike or other plant shutdown, and allocating the share granted to each in response to his perceived ratings of their product quality, dependability and technical service.

More recently, consumer marketing researchers have developed models to describe the effects and interactions of several controllable and uncontrollable variables. Some of these have been incorporated into marketing games or simulations with sufficient realism to provide a powerful teaching tool for college courses in marketing and for on-the-job training of marketing personnel. Adaptations to industrial marketing are considered in Sections F and H of this Chapter.

Advertising Models

For consumer goods, several models[9] have been developed to select the media, timing, frequency of emission and type of message for most efficient use of the advertising budget. These depend upon estimates of readership (for print) or exposure (for radio and television), threshold of effectiveness, stimulus, recall and motivation. Because the advertising of industrial goods is usually focussed on rather narrow and very specific audience segments, it seems doubtful that such models could be justified for the planning of most industrial advertising.

Distribution Models

Probably the most useful type of distribution model for marketers of industrial products is a physical distribution model[10]. It expresses total distribution cost as the sum of inventory cost (variable warehousing cost plus time value of working capital tied up in inventory), fixed warehouse cost, freight and delivery cost and the cost of lost sales and lost customers. With appropriate decision rules and programming, the model selects additional warehouse sites until no additions can be made without increasing total cost of distribution; and it eliminates sites that become uneconomical in the process.

The first three independent variables are rather easily quantified, and managerial judgment is used to estimate the cost of losing sales and customers.

A relatively simple model that minimizes computer time has been described by Kuehn and Hamburger.[11]

Sales Force Models

Division of a market geographically into sales territories usually is done intuitively by a field sales manager, based on some existing pattern for similar products.

[9] Clark and Sexton, *Marketing & Management Science: A Synergism,* Irwin, 1970,pp 271—316.
King, *Quantitative Analysis for Marketing Management,* McGraw-Hill, 1967, pp. 357—429.
Kotler, *Marketing Decision Making: A Model Building Approach,* Holt, Rinehart & Winston, 1971, pp. 428—466.
Montgomery and Urban, *Management Science in Marketing,* Prentice-Hall, 1969, pp. 137—157.
Simon and Freimer, *Analytical Marketing,* Harcourt, Brace and World, 1970, pp. 193—245.
[10] Clark and Sexton, pp. 250—66; King, pp. 512—564; Simon and Freimer, pp. 147—160.
[11] Kuehn and Hamburger, "A Heuristic Program for Locating Warehouses", *Management Science* (July, 1963), pp. 657—658.

He alters the pattern to accommodate the locations of his principal customers and prospects, using what is essentially a process of trial and error. The process can be facilitated by adapting a computerized model, derived from the transportation method of linear programming, described by Hess[12] for designing the territories of typewriter servicemen. The model assumes the salesmen want virtually equal sales workloads, that each territory must comprise only adjacent geographical sub-areas, and that each territory should be as compact as possible.

What constitutes equal sales workload will vary from one situation to another. Generally, in selling industrial products, salesmen try to call most frequently on their biggest customers, and they spend more time contacting executives. engineers or designers (i.e., selling "in depth") who may be the real decision makers or influencers within those companies. To the extent that this intention is really carried out, customer potential is an approximate measure of sales workload.

However, at least two other activities (1) calling on prospective customers, whose potential may not be known, and (2) contacting end-users for end-use development (indirect selling), would add to the workload of a salesman who is expected to develop future sales. If, in addition, the salesman will be asked to entertain certain customers outside his normal work hours (e.g., by taking a purchasing agent and his wife to dinner, or by taking the agent and his sons to a sporting event on a week-end), the estimation of sales workload becomes more complicated.

In practice, territories designed by such a method would often be only a first approximation. This would be true especially if it were desirable for a single salesman (1) to call on all customers of a specific class or industry, (2) to call on all customers who fabricate components for a certain end-user, or (3) to do indirect selling (end-use development) to the end-users served by a group of processing customers. Additional exceptions would be introduced if several large purchasers were served by a national accounts salesman, or if some of the large customers practiced centralized purchasing. Accordingly, a marketing researcher commissioned to assist in designing sales territories should first consider whether or not the number and extent of the probable exceptions might outweigh the time-saving advantage of starting with the model.

The problem of assigning salesmen to the several sales territories, also, can be approached by using a model.[13] Salesmen vary in their ability to produce sales, to convince prospects and to develop future sales applications. This might suggest devising a rating system and deliberately making territories unequal as to workload in order to present each salesman with an appropriate challenge: but it would hardly be accepted as fair by all salesmen. and the territories would have to be redesigned with each personnel change and with each major shift in economic and competitive conditions.

Some salesmen are more highly qualified than others by training and/or experience to service specific kinds of customers or specific industries. Some salesmen are

---

[12] Hess, "Realigning Districts by Computer", *Wharton Quarterly* (Spring 1969), pp. 25–30.
[13] Kotler, *Marketing Decision Making: A Model Building Approach*, Holt, Rinehart and Winston, 1971, pp. 378–379.
Clark and Sexton, *Marketing and Management Science: A Synergism*, Irwin, 1970, pp. 204-228.
Montgomery and Urban, *Management Science in Marketing*. Prentice-Hall, 1969. pp. 276–281.

more productive than others in certain geographical areas because of cultural or ethnic characteristics; and finally, some salesmen perform best where their wives are content to live. Consequently, the number of exceptions or special situations may be so large that design and redesign of the model would take more effort than intuitive solution of the assignment problem.

Several rather sophisticated models have been suggested for determining the number of calls a salesman should make on customers and prospects, the frequency and timing of his calls, the length of time he should devote to each call, and his routing or choice of sequence.[14] Their adoption by marketers of industrial goods has been rare, probably because their results have been insufficiently convincing and because exceptions to any set of general rules outweigh their advantages.

F. Simulation With an Opportunity Model

The calculation of Opportunity, described in Chapter 8, can be done by computer, although no one could justify the time and effort to write and de-bug the program if he wanted only one such calculation.

On the other hand, having collected all of the applications and their technical requirements, and having collected the properties, processing characteristics and prices of the more or less competitive candidates and incumbent products, he probably could justify the programming of a model to be used for simulation experiments. With it, he could explore the effects on Opportunity for any product of changes in

(1)   the properties of that product,
(2)   the properties of a competitive product (both
        generic and non-generic competitors),
(3)   the processing method and equipment applicable
        to one or more of the competitive products,
(4)   the price of that product (and its
        generic competitors, if any),[15]
(5)   the price of a competitive (non-generic) product,
(6)   the technical requirements of any application(s).

This gives the marketing researcher the capability of answering the "what if ...?" questions that he and his marketing managers may ask. He can easily and quickly explore the probable effects of any series of marketing strategies involving any of the six types of change listed above.

A flow chart of an Opportunity Model is shown in Figure 9–1.

The model has several uses. The marketing researcher can use it to discover the advantages of his candidate that should be emphasized by his company's sales force in their presentations to customers, and in his company's advertising, sales promotion literature and labels.

---

[14] Kotler, *Marketing Decision Making: A Model Building Approach,* Holt, Rinehart and Winston, 1971, pp. 380–407.
Montgomery and Urban, *Management Science in Marketing,* Prentice-Hall, 1969, pp.281–284.
Simon and Freimer, *Analytical Marketing,* Harcourt, Brace and World, 1970, pp. 181–190.
[15] Being realistic, we recognize that all brands of a generic product must be sold at the same price, in a normal market.

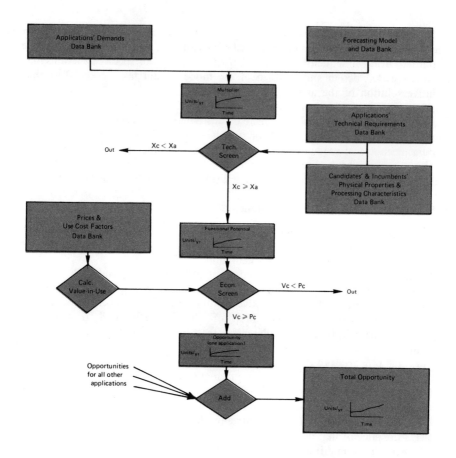

Figure 9–1. Opportunity model flow chart.

He can explore the effects on Opportunity of various hypothetical product improvements, and suggest the more important ones to his company's research personnel as worthwhile goals. With the help of the model, he can put a dollar value on each such improvement, as possible justification for the required research effort.

The model also enables the marketing researcher to discover threats from competitive products and to measure the possible losses of Opportunity that they might pose.

Finally, when a new candidate emerges, he can enter its properties and expected price into his model and quickly ascertain

○ the total Opportunity for the candidate,
○ the specific applications for which the candidate
  would be technically adequate and economically competitive,
○ the losses of Opportunity that would be suffered by each
  of the other products in his model.

If the new candidate has been developed by his own company's technical research organization (R & D), he can advise marketing management of its probable effect on earnings, and its impact on products now being marketed. With such information, management can more intelligently decide whether or not to proceed with final development and commercialization, and what changes (if any) it should then make in the rest of its product line.

If the new candidate has been introduced by a competitor, the model helps marketing management assess its threat and decide whether or not R & D should be asked to develop a counterpart.

The value of an Opportunity Model to any marketing organization depends on the economic importance of the products involved, the competitive situation, and the extent to which it is used. Creating such a model usually takes 9—12 months and costs one to two man-years of effort. Keeping it up to date may cost one or two man-months of work, each year, varying with the complexity of the model and the number of price changes, property improvements and new product entries that must be incorporated.

At present, it is believed that Opportunity Models have been constructed by only a few large companies and by one or two marketing research consultants. Simulation with Opportunity Models is one of the frontiers of marketing research. Perhaps a generalized model will be made available at a reasonable price, so that the initial cost and time would be reduced. Collecting and storing the data banks would then be the only major task, and this might cost only one-half to one man-year.

G. A Simple Example of Opportunity Simulation

In the study of markets for a new plastic resin, urea formthional, the fictitious XYZCHEM Co. mentioned in Appendix B estimated a Functional Potential of 595 million pounds per year in 1960. This was the total "demand" based solely on technical considerations.

Opportunity was then estimated, making the simplifying assumption that all fabrication and finishing costs for urea formthional (UFS) would be the same as for the incumbent thermosetting resins. Economic competitiveness was based on resin price alone, and the effect of varying the price of UFS was simulated for prices from 10 to 55 cents per pound. As expected, Opportunity for UFS increased as its price decreased to the level of one incumbent after another. For example, at 55c/lb., UFS would have had Opportunity only where high-impact melamine formaldehyde resins were used for restaurant dinnerware. At 17c/lb., UFS Opportunity was estimated to be 360 million pounds per year in 1960.

Five markets were considered in detail.

- o **Dinnerware.** Because most dinnerware was made of ceramics, it was difficult to determine price thresholds. It appeared that melamine cost more than pottery but less than quality china. The china market, then roughly 60 million pounds per year, would have become part of the UFS Opportunity at prices slightly higher than the price of melamine resins. At lower prices, UFS could have penetrated pottery applications.

o **Appliances.** The incumbent was almost exclusively phenolics, at 19–23c/lb. UFS would have begun to share that Opportunity at 20c/lb. and less, and, at 14c/lb., pick up some additional applications in which lower quality thermosets were being used.

o **Electrical and Electronics Parts.** Few possibilities appeared at UFS prices above 33c/lb., which was the price of urea formaldehyde resin. At 20c/lb., it appeared that UFS would have competed with the more expensive phenolics.

o **Screw-Cap Closures.** Really large Opportunity existed at prices low enough to compete with stamped metals; but such low prices for UFS were not foreseeable. Urea closures market would have been practical at UFS prices around 30c/lb., and phenolics could have been replaced at 20c/lb. or lower.

o **Other Markets.** Opportunity was visualized in buttons at urea formaldehyde resin prices, and in automobile parts at phenolics prices.

The specific results of these calculations are given in Table 9–1 and Figure 9–2.

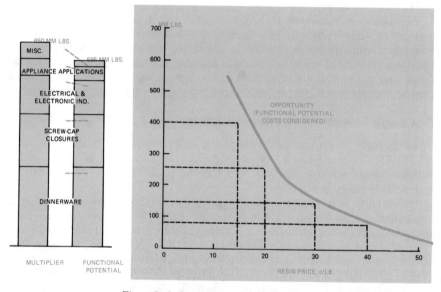

Figure 9–2. Opportunity for UFS 1960.

H. Simulation With a Marketing Strategy Model

The gap between Opportunity (demand at saturation) and forecast sales for a product can be bridged by a model that describes the effects of marketing on adoption and use of the product.

For industrial products, there are two facets to be considered:

(1) replacement of an incumbent product by the candidate product, and

(2) competition between the suppliers of the candidate product, if there are more than one manufacturer of this generic type, (see the Flow Chart in Figure 9–3).

Table 9–1. UFS Opportunity vs. Price.

UFS Price (c/lb.)	1960 OPPORTUNITY (Million Pounds per Year)					
	Appliance	Dinner-ware	Electric & Electronic	Closures	Other	Total
55	—	30	—	—	—	30
45	1	90	1	1	—	93
35	1	120	1	1	—	123
33	3	120	17	21	5	166
25	3	150	17	21	5	196
20	3	220	37	21	5	286
17	28	220	57	35	20	360
15	28	250	57	35	20	390
14	45	250	110	35	20	460
12	45	250	110	65	20	490
10	45	250	110	170	20	595

The first facet, *replacement*, must be achieved if any sales of the candidate are to be realized.[16] This is an aspect of market estimating that is generally not applicable to consumer products, and is too frequently slighted or ignored in marketing research for industrial products.

The second facet influences the *market share* enjoyed by any supplier. Together, they determine his penetration of the Opportunity, and hence his sales.

Referring to the Replacement portion of the flow chart in Figure 9–3 (upper left quadrant), we see that there are several possible incentives urging the customer to convert to the candidate product, and several restraints. It is the imbalance between these incentives and restraints that determines whether or not he replaces the incumbent. Some expansion and explanation of the brief designations of Figure 9–3 may be desirable.

(1) **Value-in-Use/Price.** This ratio of Value-in-Use (defined in Chapter 8) to price of the candidate measures the most important incentive for replacement of the incumbent.

(2) **Fringe Benefits.** In addition to the palpable savings a customer should realize from Value-in-Use, there often are intangible or smaller benefits he may find desirable, although he may not be willing to pay a premium for them. These might be aesthetic, like "depth of color" in a transparent or translucent plastic or lacquer; they might be technical, like compatibility of an electronic component with a wide range of applications; or they might be largely psychological, such as the advertising value of a trade name or manufacturer's reputation.

(3) **End-User Pull.** When indirect selling has convinced an end-user that he wants his component, sub-assembly, paint or other semi-finished article made from the candidate product, his insistence may be a potent incentive to replace the incumbent.

(4) **Availability.** A processor may hesitate to commit himself to a change if the candidate is so new that there is reasonable doubt of an adequate and dependable supply.

(5) **Prove-out.** Before deciding on a change, the processor will want not only to put the candidate through his commercial scale plant, but also to submit samples or prototypes to one or more end-users. These piloting operations, the testing required at each stage, and the return of official approvals will be time-consuming and sometimes quite expensive.

(6) **Equipment.** For major changes, the processor may have to invest in new, and perhaps unfamiliar, processing equipment or tools. Not only the capital required but also the time delay and plant outage may restrain his enthusiasm for replacement of an incumbent.

(7) **Re-training.** Before adopting the candidate, the processor may have to re-train his operators and maintenance crew. Again, both cost and time may be deterrents.

---

[16] There may be applications, previously non-existent, that are made possible and/or practical only because of properties unique to a candidate, but these are the exceptions.

(8) **End-User Resistance.** Finally, one or more of his end-users may prefer that the processor *not* change to the candidate product. His reasons may be real or imaginary, technical or psychological. They may be largely caused by inertia. Indirect selling by the supplier of the candidate product may, or may not, be sufficient to sway him.

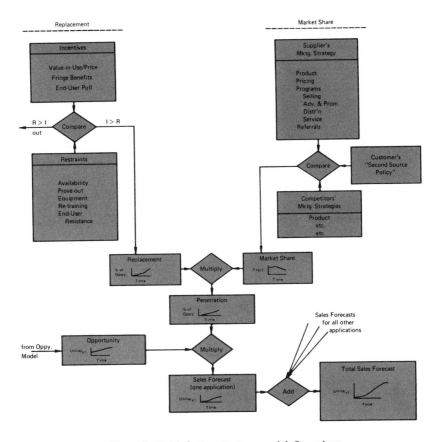

Figure 9–3. Marketing strategy model flow chart.

In the Market Share portion of the flow chart (upper right quadrant), we see that all of the elements of marketing strategy (sometimes called marketing mix) for an industrial product must be considered. The effectiveness of one supplier's strategy must be compared with that of each of his competitors, if any, who offer a generically equivalent product, (e.g., all other suppliers of Type 304 stainless steel, of a specific type of diode, of a specific grade of foamed elastomeric sheeting). Some of the elements shown deserve a bit of amplification.

(1) **Product.** Technically, we are assuming only competition-in-kind, but product quality, uniformity, dependability and small or intangible fringe benefits may be quite influential. Likewise, lead time, not only in being the first supplier, but also in developing product improvements, may give a supplier, or a competitor, much advantage.

(2) **Pricing.** In normal markets, the list prices of competitors-in-kind will necessarily be almost indistinguishable. However, the consistent price leader, the supplier who offers large, free "samples" or undercover discounts, easier terms of payment, or unusually generous credit may be rewarded with a larger market share.

(3) **Selling.** Quality of salesmen as to technical capability, personality, industriousness, persistence, attentiveness and judgment are the obvious positive factors. In some industries and in some customers' organizations, tickets to sporting events, invitations to dinner and similar extra attentions are expected and may be influential. Occasional visits or other attention by the top management of the supplier can be valuable, also. Both direct and indirect selling must be evaluated and compared with the corresponding activities of competitors.

(4) **Advertising and Promotion.** Space advertising may be less important than trade shows, promotional literature distributed by salesmen to purchasing agents and engineers, direct mail to those who influence specifications and buying decisions, and demonstrations in the customers' plants or in the supplier's sales service laboratory or model shop.

(5) **Service.** This may include technical help to solve a processor's operating problem, redesign of a component part to meet some unique requirement of a specific customer or his end-users, product development to create a marginal (and perhaps temporary) differentiation, and routine development of custom product variations (color, viscosity, surface finish, package, label, etc.)

(6) **Distribution.** Ordinarily, a customer expects only prompt and reliable delivery of just exactly the type and quantity he ordered. However, he or the supplier may suggest extras, such as inventory held by the supplier in the customer's plant from which the customer may withdraw in small quantities when needed, while being charged at truckload or other large-quantity price.

(7) **Referrals.** A supplier can usually ingratiate himself with both customers and end-users by telling end-users which of his customers are capable of supplying him, and by telling customers which end-users are preparing to request bids.

(8) **"Second Source Policy".** The meaning used here is the common one: some customers (and more end-users, especially large ones) insist on splitting their purchases between two or more suppliers as insurance against interruption of supply by strikes, fire, accident, inclement weather, etc.

The rest of the model flow chart is rather easily understood, with one word of interpretation. From the two upper quadrants down through the output rectangle labeled "Sales Forecast", we are considering one application at a time. The Opportunity output rectangle in the lower left quadrant also refers to only the same single application. Finally, the model adds the individual Sales Forecasts to get the Total Sales Forecast, symbolized in the lower right quadrant.

The mathematical expressions incorporated into the Marketing Strategy Model to relate the independent variables to the dependent variables fall into two major categories. For the Replacement portion, we want an expression according to which the fraction or percentage of Opportunity realized will be zero or very small when incentives just balance restraints, then increases slowly as the incentives begin to outweigh the restraints, increases more rapidly, then more slowly, and finally approaches 100% of Opportunity asymptotically as incentives become relatively greater and greater. For this purpose, some expression or variant of the Gompertz Function[17], such as Equation 9–1, would be appropriate.

$$Q \quad = \quad 100a^{b^x} \qquad \text{Equation 9–1}$$

where
Q	=	percentage of Opportunity realized at a point in time,
a, b	=	constants less than 1.00, and
x	=	an expression quantifying the imbalance of incentives over restraints.

For the Market Share portion of the model, an expression such as Equation 9–2, containing a variable for each of the significant elements of marketing strategy, is needed.

$$M_s \quad = \quad K \, \frac{\pi_s^a \, P_s^b \, S_s^c \cdots}{\pi_c^d \, P_c^e \, S_s^f \cdots} \qquad \text{Equation 9–2}$$

where
M_s	=	market share (a decimal fraction) enjoyed by the supplier in which we are interested,
K	=	a constant,
π_s	=	a measure of the supplier's product quality,
π_c	=	a measure of his competitors' product quality,
P_s	=	a measure of the effect of the supplier's pricing policy,
P_c	=	a measure of the effect of his competitors' pricing policies,
S_s	=	a measure of the supplier's selling effectiveness,
S_c	=	a measure of his competitors' selling effectiveness, and

$a,b,c,d,e,f\ldots$ = coefficients to be estimated.

If it should be preferred to consider the competitors individually, rather than trying to lump them together, Equation 9–3, or some variant, might be preferred.

$$M_s \quad = \quad \frac{k_s \pi_s^a \, P_s^b \, S_s^c \cdots}{\Sigma_i (k_i \, \pi_i^x \, P_i^y \, S_i^z \ldots)} \qquad \text{Equation 9–3}$$

---

[17] Kotler, *Marketing Decision Making: A Model Building Approach*, Holt, Rinehart and Winston, 1971, pp. 35–37.

where

M_s = market share (decimal fraction) enjoyed by the supplier in which we are interested,

i = the total number of competitors *and* our supplier,

$\pi_s, P_s, S_s \ldots$ = measures of the effects of the supplier's product quality, pricing policy, selling effort, etc.,

$\pi_i, P_i, S_i \ldots$ = measures of these same effects for each competitor *and* our supplier, each taken individually, and

k_i, k_s, a, b, c..x, y, z.. = constants and coefficients to be estimated.

Numerous expressions of this type have been proposed and used, primarily for forecasting market share for suppliers of consumer products.[18]

The mathematics of the remaining operations in the model is simple, involving only two multiplication steps and one addition.

The real difficulty in constructing such a model comes in attempting to quantify such complex concepts as product quality, selling effectiveness, etc. Scaling techniques, using the consensus of objective experts, have been used to develop composite ratings; and regression analysis has given values for the elasticity coefficients. Incorporating the cumulative effects of practices and performance over time presents an especially difficult problem.[19]

The construction, testing, revision and validation of such a model can require several man-years of effort, including the time of the objective experts. The magnitude of this effort and the natural skepticism of intuitive marketing managers no doubt account for the extreme paucity of Marketing Strategy Models in actual use by firms marketing industrial products.

Nevertheless, marketing researchers can hope that pioneering efforts will continue, and that the resulting techniques (especially for developing effort ratings) will be published to encourage more widespread application.

As in the case of the Opportunity Model, the most valuable contributions of Marketing Strategy Models probably have been and will be in simulation experiments to compare the relative contributions to sales and profits of the various elements of strategy. A marketing manager who had strong reason to believe that his model could tell him how much of a product improvement, for example, would counteract a competitor's pricing practices would be more confident of his decisions.

I. Venture Models

Given the Opportunity Model and a Marketing Strategy Model, it would be a logical and relatively easy task to add a Cost and Investment Model that would take known and estimated future capital investment data, operating costs, prices, etc.,

---

[18] Buzzell, Cox and Brown, *Marketing Research and Information Systems,* McGraw-Hill, 1969, p. 194.

Kotler, *Marketing Decision Making: A Model Building Approach,* Holt, Rinehart and Winston, 1971, pp. 64−80.

Montgomery and Urban, *Management Science in Marketing,* Prentice-Hall, 1969, pp. 320−323.

Sexton, "Estimating Marketing Policy Effects on Sales of a Frequently Purchased Product", *J. Marketing Research,* Vol. VII (Aug. 1970), pp. 338−347.

[19] Amstutz, *Computer Simulation of Competitive Market Response,* M.I.T. Press, 1967.

plus the sales forecasts from the second model and calculate earnings, return on investment, and other financial measures of the business.

The resulting combination would be a Venture Model, combining internal and external facts, estimates and programs into an integrated picture of a business venture.

Such a Venture Model was described in broad outline by Armstrong[20] for application to the carpet yarn business.

Here also, simulation would probably be the most productive use in the next several years. However, as models were refined and accepted, one can visualize the possibility that a really complete model would not only answer questions, such as

(1) "What will be the probable effect on company earnings growth if we introduce a new product having such and such characteristics?",

but that the interrogation might be made in reverse by asking

(2) "What are the properties and necessary selling price of a product that might add $10 million per year to our earnings by the eighth year after introduction?", or

(3) "What must we do about product line, product quality, pricing, selling effectiveness, and so on to raise our earnings to $50 million per year by ten years from now?"

One of the important characteristics of an effective marketing researcher is a well-developed imagination, so that he may visualize how model building might help him to do a more effective job for his clients, the marketing managers.

EXERCISES

1. Choose a product (material, component part, supply or piece of equipment) or a service, and imagine that you plan to design a marketing information system for a company that would supply it. List
    ○ the management personnel who might receive reports
    ○ the kinds of decisions they must make
    ○ the categories of information they would need in
    order to make those decisions.
2. Design the output reports for each of the managers visualized in (1) above.
3. List the specific types and probable sources of input data needed for (1) and (2) above.
4. Imagine that you are a marketing researcher for a manufacturer of temperature-sensing devices. Assume there are 6 or 7 competitors and hundreds of customers whose applications could be arranged into 8 or 10 broad categories, such as (1) very low temperature, (2) very high temperatures, (3) moderate temperature in corrosive atmosphere, (4) high temperature under high pressure, etc. Suppose you knew the total number of sensing devices installed in a recent year, had a rather reliable estimate of the percentage distribution between the 8 or 10 categories, and knew the approximate production capacity of each competitor. Suppose, further, that you had reason

---

[20] Howard I. Armstrong, "Marketing Research and the Growing Carpet Industry", Chemical Marketing Research Assn., Paper No. 635, Washington, D.C., Meeting, Feb. 12–14, 1969.

to believe that you knew how many Type 1 devices were sold by competitors C, F and G, how many Type 3 devices were sold by B, D and F, but no other market share information (except, of course, that of your own company).

Devise a system and write a flow chart for a model that would allocate "unsatisfied demand" for each type of device among the competitors having "unused capacity", and thus calculate market share, by application, for all of the 6 or 7 competitors, assuming

(1)   that all your competitors are equally capable of producing devices meeting the technical requirements of each application category, *or*

(2)   that certain competitors are preferred suppliers of one or more types, and certain other competitors are virtually incapable of supplying one or more types.

5.   Starting with an estimate of Opportunity made in response to Exercise 3, Chapter 8, simulate the effects on Opportunity of changes in properties, prices, technical requirements and/or processing equipment.

CHAPTER 10

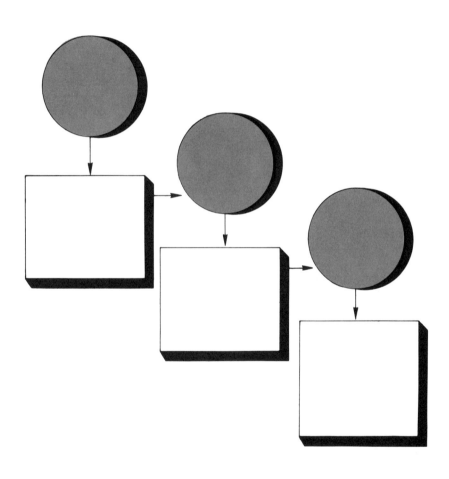

SPECIAL SERVICES OF MARKETING RESEARCH

Principal among the other services that can be performed by marketing researchers eager to help their clients in the marketing organization are these four.

- Decision Trees, to assist in selecting among alternatives in marketing strategy
- Critical Path Diagrams, to help schedule and monitor progress toward the commercialization of a new product
- Market Testing and Concept Testing, to explore and evaluate the suitability of a proposed new product
- End-Use Development, or indirect selling, to assist end-users in visualizing and evaluating applications of a material or subassembly made with a product offered by the marketing researcher's company.

A. Decision Trees

Although they were developed many years ago and have been used quite successfully by a few companies, decision trees are not in widespread use in marketing. There may be many reasons for this. Many texts describing the technique[1] have gone rapidly and deeply into rather complex expositions of statistical theory that are not understood by many marketing managers; and some of the examples cited have dealt with decisions relating to oil well drilling or manufacturing, rather than with marketing.

In marketing practice, much value can be obtained by using the simplest form of decision tree. A marketing manager (encouraged and assisted by his marketing researcher) who agrees to try it, is (1) led to visualize each of the principal alternatives he may be facing, and (2) required to make his best estimates of the probabilities that these alternatives might be realized. Even if he barely understands "expected monetary value", he is likely to understand his *problem* more clearly than before.

There are those who argue that the subjective probabilities assigned in making decision trees are unreal; i.e., that there is no such thing as the numerical probability of an event that has not occurred. There is no doubt, however, that anyone making a logical choice between alternatives does estimate the relative likelihood of one versus another, even if he is not conscious of doing so. Therefore, it would seem that a technique that brings those estimates out for critical examination ought to generate better decisions.

A simplified decision tree is shown in Figure 10–1 to illustrate how the technique might be applied. The fictitious chemical company, XYZCHEM Co., is assumed to be supplying plastic molding resins to a customer who requests a special modification he believes will help him bid successfully for a new custom molding contract from one of his larger customers (an end-user in the perspective of

[1] Cox and Enis, *The Marketing Research Process*, Good year, 1972, pp. 423–460.
Green and Tull, *Research for Marketing Decisions*, Prentice-Hall, 2nd ed., 1970, pp. 39–71.
Kotler, *Marketing Decision Making: A Model Building Approach*, Holt, Rinehart and Winston, 1971, pp. 257–284.
Raiffa and Schlaifer, *Applied Statistical Decision Theory*, Harvard Business School, 1961.

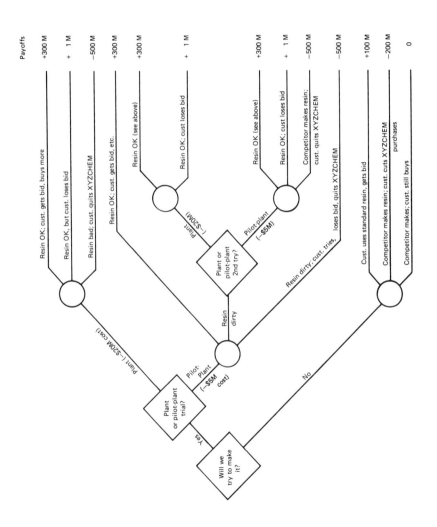

Figure 10–1. Decision tree for special resin.

XYZCHEM). Choices that might be made by XYZCHEM management are shown at the diamond-shaped spaces and events not under control of XYZCHEM emanate from the circles. Estimated payoffs are given in the final column.

Beginning at the diamond labeled "Will we try to make it?", let us follow the upper branch, to explain the full meaning of designations that are somewhat abbreviated in Figure 10–1. Immediately after the decision to make the resin, XYZCHEM faces another decision; i.e., whether to produce a trial lot in full commercial plant equipment or in a pilot plant. The costs are indicated as being $20,000 and $5,000, respectively. Following the upper branch, further, which assumes a full-scale plant trial, we come to the circle where the branch divides to show three possible outcomes (the uncontrolled events):

(1)   The resin is satisfactory, the customer molds his prototypes, submits his bid, is awarded the contract, and is so pleased that he not only buys $100,000 worth of the new resin but also increases his purchases of other resins from XYZCHEM by $200,000. The payoff is the increased revenues to XYZCHEM over the base case ($800,000-$500,000 = $300,000).

(2)   The resin is satisfactory, but the customer loses the contract to a competitor for some reason not attributable to actions of XYZCHEM. Here it is assumed that the only payoff is the scrap value of unused trial resin.

(3)   The resin is faulty for some reason, the customer loses the contract, and he retaliates against XYZCHEM by discontinuing all purchases. This gives a negative payoff.

Beginning again at "Will we try to make it?", let us assume the decision is, "Yes, but in the pilot plant", and look at the central part of the tree. At the circle, we again have three uncontrolled events. The uppermost shows success and the same $300,000 payoff as in subparagraph (1), above. The lowest branch shows failure and retaliation as in (3), above. The middle branch shows a second choice between full plant and pilot plant trials, with suggested possible outcomes and payoffs similar to those already described.

In the bottom-most portion of the tree, we have an assumed decision not to make and supply a trial lot of the special resin. The suggested possible outcomes (from top to bottom) are

(1)   The customer uses a standard XYZCHEM resin, gets the contract, and increases his purchases by just enough to produce against that contract, giving XYZCHEM a payoff of $100,000.

(2)   A competitor of XYZCHEM produces a special resin, and is rewarded by the customer, giving XYZCHEM a negative payoff.

(3)   A competitor makes a special resin, but the customer is loyal to XYZCHEM to the extent of continuing his usual level of purchases.

Figure 10–2 shows the same decision tree with the addition of probabilities assigned to the uncontrolled events by the marketing management of XYZCHEM. At each circle, it also shows the expected monetary value of the group of events emanating from each circle. For example, at the circle in the uppermost branch, we have written in "+ $130.3 M", which is the sum of the three products of probability times payoff (in this case, $0.6 \times \$300 M + 0.3 \times \$1 M - 0.1 \times \$500 M = \$130.3 M$). When the cost of the plant trial batch has been subtracted, the expected

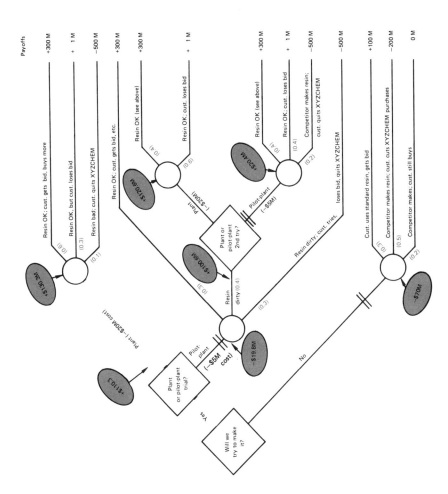

Payoffs

Resin OK; cust. gets bid, buys more — +300 M
Resin OK, but cust. loses bid — + 1 M
Resin bad; cust. quits XYZCHEM — –500 M
Resin OK; cust. gets bid, etc. — +300 M
Resin OK (see above) — +300 M
Resin OK, cust. loses bid — + 1 M
Resin OK (see above) — +300 M
Resin OK, cust. loses bid — + 1 M
Competitor makes resin; cust. quits XYZCHEM — –500 M
loses bid, quits XYZCHEM — –500 M
Cust. uses standard resin, gets bid — +100 M
Competitor makes resin; cust. cuts XYZCHEM purchases — –200 M
Competitor makes; cust. still buys — 0 M

Figure 10–2. Decision tree for special resin (with probabilities).

monetary value of that branch of the tree is + $110.3 M. Doing the same thing for all other branches, we find that a decision to make the resin in full plant equipment appears to be the wisest choice.

To see how the decision might have been affected by a different set of assumed probabilities, see Figure 10–3. The probabilities in this case are generally less favorable to taking the largest risk, and are less optimistic of easy success. They are typical of the judgments of more conservative, or perhaps skeptical, management. In this case the wisest decision would seem to be to gain experience in pilot plant before risking a full plant trial.

Not all cases are this simple, of course, but many are; and a marketing researcher can be of service to his marketing manager by being ready to sketch out a decision tree (preferably on the back of an envelope, on the spot) whenever the manager says "I've got a puzzling decision to make. What can you do to help me?"

B. Critical Path Diagrams

Planning for the introduction of a new product usually involves many activities on the part of many sub-organizations. Not only must production facilities be made available, and an inventory of the new product be accumulated for the first commercial shipments. Final details of manufacturing may remain to be worked out, tests of the product may be needed to complete evaluation and to provide information to be incorporated into product data sheets and advertising, market testing in commercial facilities of a selected few customers usually will be desirable, and salesmen may need to be trained.

After plans have been laid out and tasks have been assigned, it will invariably be desirable to monitor progress of the tasks against schedule to avoid or minimize the detrimental effects of delays. A diagram such as that in Figure 10–4 can be very useful to a marketing manager or his staff assigned to coordinate the total project, for they can see at a glance what will be required. If they also add notations to the chart as each task is completed, they can easily detect undesirable lags and explore corrective actions.

Such a chart can also be used in task force meetings with representatives of manufacturing, engineering, R & D, etc., as the work proceeds. Finally, it may be most useful in showing top management what progress has been made.

Figure 10–5 illustrates an alternative form that has the advantage of making the time deadlines more readily perceived. It has the disadvantage of being practical only in projects involving relatively few tasks.

Critical path techniques have become fairly standard for construction, manufacturing and some development organizations. They have rarely been used in marketing. Marketing researchers could lead the way toward more general application to marketing projects, rendering another service to management.

C. Market Testing

Marketing researchers are the logical persons to probe their markets for product acceptance. Such probing can take various forms, depending on the type of product and its stage of development.

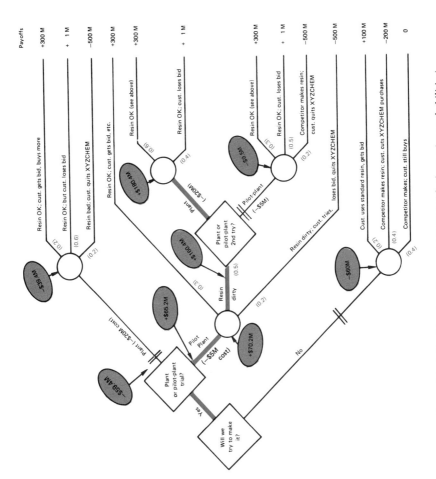

Figure 10–3. Decision tree for special resin (with alternative probabilities).

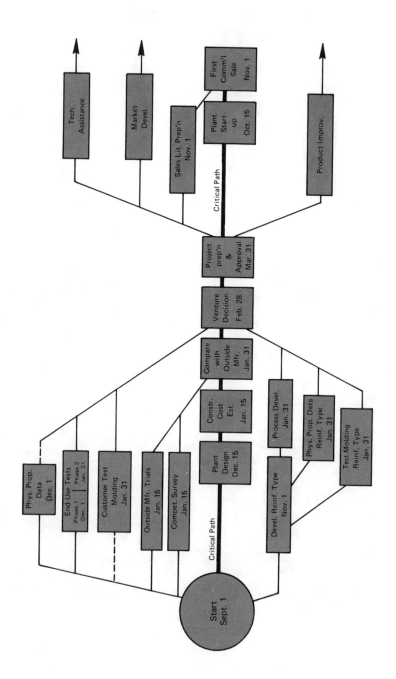

Figure 10–4. Critical path diagram for a new product.

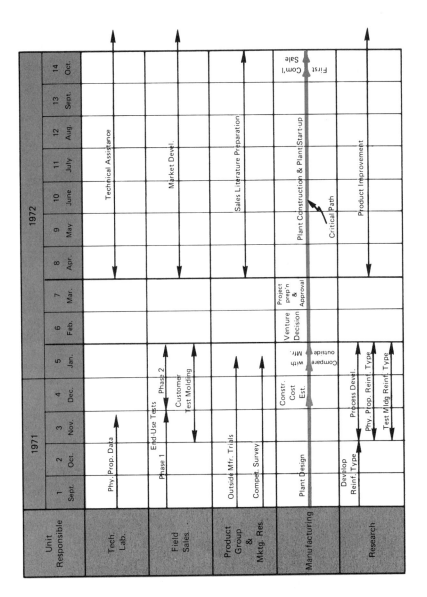

Figure 10–5. Critical path chart for new product.

If the product is still in the idea stage, the technique of *concept testing* is as appropriate for industrial products as for consumer products. It may be the only way to evaluate a new product if the firm can not afford to build a pilot-plant or make a full-scale model. A number of experts (usually customers) are shown tentative specifications, drawings and/or rough prototypes of a new component part, or physical properties, laboratory samples, and/or test specimens of a raw material. They are asked for critical comments and suggestions for improving the candidate. More important, they are asked to visualize applications for the candidate.

Candidate products that have progressed further may be subjected to various forms of *use testing*. These preferably involve practical applications in full-scale plant equipment to produce commercial intermediate or end-products. For example, (1) a new source of illumination would be substituted for standard light bulbs in the instrument panels of several hundred radios made on the usual assembly line, (2) a new die-casting alloy would be substituted for bronze in casting a plumbing valve body in a commercial die-casting shop, (3) a candidate unsaturated carboxylic acid would be substituted for acrylic acid in making a paint latex in a full-scale polymerization kettle. Whatever the specific case, the objective is to get some measure of acceptance by the customer, and sometimes by the end-user as well. This may involve extensive laboratory and/or practical use tests of the fabricated product.

Marketing researchers engaged in any form of market testing need sufficient knowledge of the technical aspects of products, processing (or fabrication) and end-use to discuss these intelligently with their customers' engineers and scientists. They should also be well versed in interviewing techniques. In concept testing, they may find it desirable to send their respondents some written description for study before the interview. In use testing, the supplier may find it necessary to pay a customer for machine time or for standard production lost during the test.

This is not the place for exhaustive discussion, but it should be mentioned in passing, that there may be compelling reasons for trying to keep all aspects of market testing confidential for as long as possible to prevent competitors from copying the candidate. Thus, concept testing and use testing might be undertaken with a select few, highly-trusted customers, only. Use testing might be done under terms of a so-called development contract, to formalize the agreement to maintain confidence; furthermore, the supplier might gather up all sub-assemblies, processed materials, and un-used candidate product to prevent them from reaching competitors.

Market testing is used to evaluate the suitability (especially the technical adequacy) of a candidate. Any confirmation it may give of the marketing researcher's estimate of demand is, of course, welcome; but it should never be used as the principal source of demand estimation, because of the limited number of customers involved.

A related activity, *test marketing,* involves offering a new product for sale and use, usually in a geographically limited area, to gauge national demand by scaling up the test results. The technique is rather commonly used on consumer goods, for which it may be the only reliable way to estimate total demand. It is seldom used on industrial goods because (1) it announces the candidate to competitors through the purchasing agents' grapevine, and (2) there may be no representative geographic area, as the processing firms are rarely dispersed evenly. Furthermore, there may be no way to produce enough of the candidate for commercial sale without committing the capital investment and construction time for a full-scale plant. An exception to this rule is the case of an unavoidable by-product, which may be offered widely in the hope that some potential customer may discover a use for it. There is reason, however, to doubt the effectiveness of advertisements and salesmen's pitches that, in effect, say, "We don't know what this is good for. What can *you* do with it?"

D. End-Use Development

End-use development, or indirect selling, is the process of showing an end-user the advantages of specifying that a certain candidate product be used by the processor or fabricator who makes an intermediate or sub-assembly for him. For example, a supplier of a plastic molding resin might convince a manufacturer or electric motors to try bearings made of his resin, rather than of bronze, pointing to dollar savings and perhaps to quieter motor operation as expected benefits. If he succeeds, the end-user's *pull* adds to the resin salesman's *push* as incentive to the bearing maker.

Although large suppliers usually assign this responsibility to End-Use Technologists, it may be another function of the marketing researcher in a smaller firm.

EXERCISES

1. Visualize a problem in the marketing of an industrial product, in which several alternatives are possible, and draw a decision tree for it. Calculate expected monetary value for each possible alternative, using assumed payoffs and probabilities, to find the preferred solution. Change the probabilities and recalculate to show the effect on preferred solution.

2. Draw a critical path diagram or chart for commercialization of a real or fictional new product.

3. Imagine you are the marketing researcher assigned to market test a new product or service. Outline the steps you would take to (1) select customers to do the testing, (2) conduct the test, and (3) evaluate the results.

4. Pick a product for which indirect selling might be appropriate. Assuming that this might be done by either marketing researchers or technical sales personnel, describe the advantages and disadvantages, to the supplier, of having it done by marketing researchers. What benefits might accrue to the marketing researchers?

CHAPTER 11

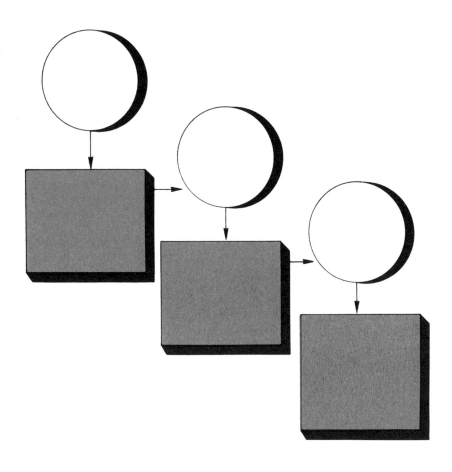

INTERNATIONAL MARKETING RESEARCH

The principles and techniques of industrial marketing research should be universally applicable; but there are practical limitations outside the United States that vary from one country to another. The limitations fall into four major categories:
(1) the relative shortage of reliable published statistics,
(2) the often powerful influence of governments on trade,
(3) the varying proportion of population that participates in the money economy, and
(4) the complications of communications in many countries.

A. Published Statistics

North Americans, who are accustomed to abundant and generally reliable data published by government and trade organizations, find the relative scarcity of such data abroad to be disconcerting at best, and discouraging in general. The needed figures are often simply not recorded, and those that are published may be of doubtful accuracy. Even in Western Europe, trade association data may be incomplete, for a major producer may not be a member of the association.[1]

Differences in definitions and units between countries preclude simple addition to get accurate totals for a multinational region; and the relatively high proportion of exports and imports results in major discrepancies between production and consumption in almost any country.

The result is a need for much more inquiry from primary sources, especially in the less well developed countries of Latin America, Asia and Africa. This should be preceded, or course, by a thorough search of the secondary sources available at home, such as the *Statistical Year Book*, issued by the United Nations, the many reports prepared by multinational banks, and especially the increasingly extensive and reliable "Overseas Business Reports" series published by the U.S. Department of Commerce. The books, *A Basic Guide to Exporting* and *Selling in Europe,* as well as the periodical, *Commerce Today*[2], contain much valuable background information.

A marketing researcher can only sift the evidence from all sources, cross-check and double-check by visiting government and industry sources, or by searching out additional sources. He may find that a few thousand dollars paid to a local marketing research consulting firm is a better investment than more money spent for his travel and living expenses abroad. Good consultants are becoming available in Europe, and they may be located by direct inquiry or through the offices of the American Management Association, the American Marketing Association or the Chemical Marketing Research Association.

---

[1] For an extensive list and discussion of secondary sources, see Giragosian (ed.), *Chemical Marketing Research,* Reinhold, 1967, Chapter 11, pp. 262–282.
[2] *A Basic Guide to Exporting,* U.S. Dept. of Commerce, 1974(?). Deschampsneufs, *Selling in Europe,* London Business Publications, 1963.
Commerce Today, (monthly), U.S. Dept. of Commerce.

B. Government Influences

The consumption of a product may bear little relation to true demand in countries with balance of payments problems so pressing as to require direct restraint of imports. This usually is true also when a struggling local manufacturer is given protection from imports. The effects are to distort not only demand but also price, making it very difficult and risky to predict either one beyond the immediate future.

Conversely, governments sometimes strongly encourage foreign investment by giving tax and other financial incentives, as Brazil has done to encourage development of its northeastern states. In such cases, access to such statistics as may be available, and entree to primary sources can be greatly facilitated by friendly government officials.

Even with the best of good will toward industry and commerce, a government may distort its economy and inhibit normal development by imposing arbitrary limits on raw materials, restrictions on employment of aliens, tariffs on imports and exports, and taxes on plant, equipment, inventory and working capital, in addition to income taxes.

Worse than the existence of such restraints, however, is the probability that they will change with little or no advance notice, especially in the politically less stable countries and in the socialist dictatorships.

C. Demographic Variables

The relationship between population and the consumption of industrial goods and services varies enough between North America, Western Europe, the United Kingdom, Australia, New Zealand, and Japan to present estimating problems. Beyond those areas, however, the relationship frequently breaks down completely, and a marketing researcher must ascertain what proportion of a country's population has risen above the subsistence level and is therefore contributing to the economy. The proportion may be surprisingly low, even in economically progressive countries such as Brazil, where the effective buying population was estimated recently to be between 10 and 15% of the total population, depending upon the type of product.

Religion, tradition and other cultural characteristics can be even more influential than economics, especially in Asia, the Middle East and Africa. Dietary and other preferences have direct influences on purchases of consumer goods, and indirect effects on the raw materials, components, supplies, services and equipment that might be precursors to those consumer goods.

Finally, some peoples, having been conditioned by centuries of struggle against an ungenerous terrain, have become more energetic and frequently more open to the introduction of new products than are those living where food is easy to find and/or grow.

Consequently, marketing research abroad must consider these variables for each specific country and sometimes for geographical regions within a country (e.g., India).

D. Communications

Automatically, one thinks of the language barriers in contemplating interviews abroad; but the actual barriers are not impassable in most European and the larger Latin American countries, for many industrialists and other educated individuals speak excellent English. Some of them even resist speaking their native languages because they are eager to practice speaking English.

There is, however, always an advantage in being able to at least open the interview and conduct the polite formalities in the respondent's language. This can be of considerable help in establishing rapport and setting up an informal, comfortable atmosphere for the interview. Further, if the visiting marketing researcher really is fluent, he can catch innuendoes in the comments that may be passed between two or more respondents during the interview. (Incidentally, it has been observed that it is a significant advantage to carry and distribute freely business cards on which the visitor's title is given in the local language.)

Interpreters can be hired in almost any country, especially in the larger cities (where most interviews would ordinarily be held), and they can be most helpful in interviewing smaller firms located away from the large industrial centers. However, finding an interpreter who not only understands English but also understands the technology may be impossible. Therefore, a marketing researcher should avail himself of the services of a sales representative or distributor if this is practicable.

A good local representative or distributor offers much more than understanding of the technology and language, for he can be invaluable in helping select informed respondents and in arranging appointments. If he is reliable and well-known, his intervention will set the stage for a productive interview.

Almost invariably, the initial contacts with potential respondents must be made by letter, far in advance of the visits. This greatly increases the probability that the intended respondent will be available, gives him a chance to prepare for the interview, and makes it easier to establish an itinerary without back-tracking and costly delays en route. If the distributor or other local representative should be willing, he can be of tremendous help with these arrangements; and he can provide background information on the respondent companies and supplement their data with a perspective that the visiting marketing researcher would never acquire in a single trip. Furthermore, he may be able to furnish key pieces of information that were overlooked during the interviews.

The protocol of arranging interviews is even stricter abroad than in the United States.[3] The first contact must be made with top management, usually the Managing Director, for until he authorizes someone to answer specific questions, the respondent will not go beyond polite generalities. A personal interview with the Managing Director may be necessary; and when he has given authorization, his designated expert respondent may be surprisingly frank and open. The interviewer, also, should be prepared to give information in exchange, even if it must be limited to aggregates and trends (e.g., data on markets in the United States).

---

[3] Roger Williams, Jr., *Technical Market Research,* Roger Williams Technical & Economic Services, S.A., Geneva, Switzerland, 1962, pp. 69—71.

Travel abroad can be difficult and tiring, hotel accommodations are not always to one's liking, and telephone service is sometimes plainly inadequate. Yet, with only sparse published information, a personal visit is likely to be the most satisfying alternative. Good planning and the help of a local representative are imperative for best results.

EXERCISE

1 Choose a foreign country and an industrial product. Gather data on population, gross domestic product (GDP), total manufacturing output, exports and imports of manufactured goods, and especially such data as may be available on demand for an aggregate that might include your chosen industrial product. Estimate probable consumption of the chosen product, and compare it with any available data on consumption of that specific product.

A Company Profile

The following is a profile of a fictional company, Roxco Corporation, assumed to be a customer of another fictional company, XYZCHEM Co., which supplies pigments to Roxco.

ROXCO CORPORATION

General Description — This company is one of the largest regional paint manufacturers in the Western states, with products in industrial as well as the usual retail trade lines. Through subsidiaries, it is a national supplier of printers' inks, sign paints, artists' supplies and art materials for schools and institutions.

Organization — The parent company headquarters offices are at 5500 Ventura Ave., Ventura, Calif. 93001, on the site of the main paint plant. District sales offices are located in Eureka and Sacramento, Calif., Flagstaff, Ariz., Boise, Idaho, Eugene, Oregon, Ogden, Utah, and Everett, Wash.

Principal officers of the company are shown in the partial organization chart and discussed below.

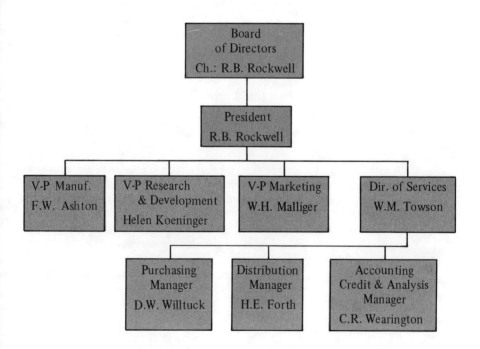

Chairman and President:

R. B. Rockwell was the original entrepreneur and founder, and is still the financial genius of the company and its subsidiaries. Although he spends more time now on his yacht, based in nearby Hueneme Marina, he seems to come back from each trip with a new idea to expand the company's operations, acquire a new subsidiary or arrange for rights to a new invention. I would guess he is in his late fifties. He is believed to hold approximately 25% of the parent company's common stock and 25% of the preferred. Known as "RB", even by his paper-boy.

V-P Manufacturing:

Ed Ashton, one of the 5 original partners with Rockwell, has run the paint plants since he designed the first in a one-story vacated warehouse on Mission Street. He sticks pretty closely to investment and operating matters, is a tyrant on quality control, and stays away from anything related to marketing, if he can. Age, perhaps 62. May own 15% of preferred stock, very little of the common.

V-P Research and Development:

Helen Koeninger, RB's first wife, is known by associates as "The Dynamo" for her innovative (sometimes shocking) ideas for new and improved products, and her challenges to the rest of the Board members to get into novel product lines. She takes little interest in the paint business, except to approve the annual "new color selections". In fact, she has urged dropping the retail paint business, saying it has been only marginally profitable, even in good years. Openly admits she is 57 and occasionally brags of owning just a few more shares of common stock than her ex-husband. She is now married to Jay Koeninger, a local commercial artist, politician and one-time mayor of Ventura.

V-P Marketing:

Bill Malliger is on the road so much of the time, in and out of the District Sales Offices, and conferring with the marketing managers of the subsidiary companies that he is hardly more than a legend to employees outside of the Board and his Marketing Department. At the same time, he keeps informed so well that it is allegedly he, more than RB, who makes Roxco a truly market-oriented outfit; and he comes closer to being the first assistant president than the other V-Ps in terms of business judgment and corporate policy influence. Being only 45, or so, he is said to be a good prospect for promotion to president when RB releases his grip a little (as he threatens to do, more and more often). Nobody seems to know how much stock he owns; and it may not be much, for he joined the original five partners after their venture was launched.

Director of Services:

Walter Towson, about 63, another of the original partners, seems to be the steadying influence in the company. He has a phenomenal memory for figures and a quiet way of bringing the others back to reality when the Board begins to "dream out loud" about a new opportunity. At the same time, he is not stodgy, but can get rather enthusiastic about a business proposition he thinks is sound. Runs a very orderly shop. Believed to hold 10–15% of the common and 35% of preferred stock.

Purchasing Manager:

Dave Willtuck is our principal contact and loyal friend. He is open to suggestion, interested in new products, and cooperative in supplying inventory data, demand forecasts and entree to the rest of the organization. He also knows the buyers in the subsidiaries and has been influential in getting XYZCHEM some significant chunks of their purchases, although he has no official jurisdiction over them. Probably in his late thirties. Says he is trying to buy company stock from any officer willing to sell, but hasn't acquired much, yet.

Accounting, Credit and Analysis Manager:

Charles R. Wearington is the thorn in our side, and has been ever since the "1961 incident", (see History, below) which alienated any affection he might have had for XYCHEM at that time. He never lets our credit division, or sales representatives, forget what an important and stable company Roxco is. If we ever have a repetition of 1961, we'll never get through Roxco's front door again, until Wearington retires — and that will not occur for another seven years. May own 5–10% of the preferred stock.

Comment:

Rockwell, Ashton, Koeninger, Towson and a man named Giddings were the original five partners. Giddings was an inventor who lost interest in an idea as soon as he proved it would work. He left the company early, but is reported to be holding a few shares of common stock "just for old time's sake".

The formal relationship between Roxco and its subsidiaries is shown in this chart.

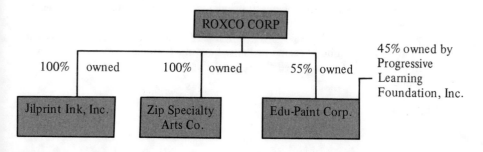

Jilprint Ink, Inc., as the name implies, is the maker of printing ink, including rotogravure and other specialty and "glossy" (high style) inks. It also supplies color concentrates to formulators ·of plastics, elastomers, ball-point pen inks, etc. Main office, 12399 Montecito Way, Santa Barbara, Calif. 93103. Principal officers: President, B. B. Schoetting; V-P Marketing, Helen Koeninger; Manufacturing Manager, Juan Martinez; Finance Director, Roberto Lopez; Principal Buyer, W. P. Alpin. Mrs. Koeninger is the main source of ideas, new products and sales efforts. Bill Alpin buys what she wants and Juan needs. We have very cordial relations, here, and enjoy probably 75% of Jilprint's pigment purchases.

Zip Specialty Arts Co. is Helen Koeninger's pride and joy. It was her idea to do a superior job for artists in providing oil, watercolor, fresco and (now) acrylic paints, plus brushes, etc., and the equipment for etching and lithography – all in ready-to-use condition and convenience-packaged. Commercial spray paints for trans-illuminated acrylic signs, bronzing lacquers, silk-screening inks and other specialties have been added, over the years, to the point where Zip is internationally recognized. Domestic sales cover the U.S. Exports are handled through many import-export houses, both U.S.-based and foreign. Main office: 42 Paso Robles, Ojai, Calif. 93023. Principal officers: President, Helen Koeninger; Director of Marketing and Design, Esmerelda Esperanza; Manufacturing Manager, Jose Martin; Accounting and Purchasing, Arch Dwyer. If Dwyer buys pigments from any firm except XYZCHEM, he must smuggle the stuff into the plant in his briefcase.

Edu-Paint Corp. is a jointly owned subsidiary in which Progressive Learning Foundation, Inc., holds 45% interest and has been the source of money, innovation and inspiration. It has also supplied access to institutional customers. Roxco supplied the manufacturing, marketing and financial know-how. To date the firm has been just holding its own, financially, against some of the older and larger competitors. Main offices: 246 Filbert St., San Francisco, Calif. 94101. Principal officers: President, Dr. George Schultz (who is also president of Progressive Learning); Marketing V-P, W. H. Malliger; Manufacturing and Engineering Director, Enrico Hudd; Buyer, John Jones. Except for a very few metallic pigments for decorative and sign inks, Edu-Paint does not buy pigments, directly. Almost all of its paint, lacquer, etc., is bought in fully-formulated condition from Roxco. I think XYZCHEM gets at least 40% of the pigment orders placed by Edu-Paint, such as they are.

Manufacturing Locations

Roxco Corp.

Main Plant: 5500 Ventura Ave., Ventura, Calif. 93001
Others: Alden Road, Red Bluff, Calif. 96080
              Highway 64, Red Lake, Ariz. 86014
              993 Mukilteo Highway, Everett, Wash. 98203

Jilprint Ink, Inc.

Ink Plant: 14,430 Bristol Road, Warren, R.I. 02885
Concentrates: 4001 Highway 202, Danbury, Conn. 06810

ROXCO CORPORATION

Zip Specialty Arts Co.

Artists' Materials: 4900 Asilomar Drive, Montery, Calif. 93940
                           Route 100, Chadd's Ford, Pa. 19346
Commercial: 737 Hayes Blvd., Fremont, Ohio 43551

Edu-Paint Corp.

Plant and Warehouse: Santa Cruz Highway, Half Moon Bay, Calif. 94019.

History – Besides what has been said and implied above, these facts are important.

Rockwell, Helen Koeninger (then Mrs. Rockwell), Ashton, Giddings and Towson founded the parent company as Southern California Paint and Varnish Company, in 1941, just in time to get some very large orders for new and re-fitted naval vessels. With the profits from WW II business, the company expanded its retail trade line, consolidated its industrial line, flirted briefly with automotive enamels and lacquers in 1950–57, and built its large, main plant out Ventura Avenue toward the oil field, during the latter part of 1951.

Zip Specialties was established in 1958, apparently with much fanfare (cocktail parties for artists in Carmel and San Francisco, sponsored art shows in Los Angeles, Washington, D.C., etc.).

Jilprint was purchased in 1960, for $7 million in cash, from B.B. Schoetting and his associates, who had established and run the firm as Rhode Island Tinte Ltd. from 1939 until the acquisition. Only Schoetting remains active, the other former principals having gone into retirement.

With the purchase of Jilprint on top of the excesses of Zip, came not only RB's divorce from Helen but also financial difficulties that led XYZCHEM and several other suppliers to withdraw the usual credit terms and insist on strictly C.O.D. shipments for ten or eleven months in late 1960 and the first half of 1961. A minor reorganization under a new name, Roxco Corp., a major loan from Wells Fargo, and a lot of hard work got Roxco back into a profitable position by July or August, 1961. A very shrewd bargain, made much earlier with RB, left Helen with 20% of the company's common stock and a position from which even divorce could not shake her.

The financial repercussions and the maneuvering required to recover increased Wearington's stature as a prophet and as a diplomatic negotiator with bankers. All of this also made him very hard-nosed with Roxco's suppliers, especially those who, like XYZCHEM, had been hard-nosed with him in 1961.

Financial Information – Because Roxco is so closely held, no annual report is published. The following figures have been gleaned from a Dun & Bradstreet sheet and conversations with several of the officers.

	1975	1974
Net Sales, Roxco and wholly-owned subsidiaries	110,730,000	100,125,000
Net income (ditto)	11,622,000	9,564,000

Appendix A

BALANCE SHEET
ROXCO CORP. AND WHOLLY-OWNED SUBSIDIARIES

ASSETS	1975	1974
Current Assets	104,000,000	86,000,000
Property Plant and Equipment, less Depreciation	11,000,000	13,000,000
Patents, goodwill, etc.	5,000,000	7,000,000
Total	120,000,000	106,000,000

LIABILITIES		
Current Liabilities	48,000,000	39,000,000
Long-term debt	19,000,000	27,000,000
Stockholders' Equity	53,000,000	40,000,000
Total	120,000,000	106,000,000

Development and Expansion Plans — Jilprint needs ink and concentrates plants in the Middle-West and on the Pacific Coast. Juan Martinez, Manufacturing Manager, and his engineers are said to be negotiating through an engineering consulting firm for sites with suitable buildings in place. Bill Alpin, the Buyer, estimates an increase of 50% in our pigments sales when the plants are running (perhaps 2 years from now).

Zip will expand its commercial plant (making sign paints, screening inks, etc.) at Fremont, Ohio, later this year, to double its present capacity — and we expect to double our sales.

Roxco R & D, under Helen Koeninger, has been devoting much time to a very confidential project. According to the grapevine, it will require a new plant in Northern California or Oregon; but no one talks about the product(s). All we have been able to learn from Dave Willtuck, Purchasing Manager, is that new pigments will be required. He won't say whether he means new to Roxco, or new to XYZCHEM. Our Sales Representative, Rosco Barnes, is making frequent inquiry so as to give our Research Lab. as much advance notice as possible of any technical development that may be needed.

Corporate Policies and Reputation — Dun and Bradstreet gives Roxco high praise for consistent performance, prompt payment of obligations and ethical dealing. The few Roxco customers we have contacted, including Peerless Sign Co., Amono Appliances, Pegasus Publishing Co., have invariably spoken highly of Roxco, Jilprint and Edu-Paint for quality products and fair dealing. Zip has an outstanding reputation among the artist colonies of Carmel, Cape Cod and Bar Harbor, Maine, for innovative products, in spite of its higher prices.

117

ROXCO CORPORATION

Since its debacle of 1960–61, Roxco and wholly-owned subsidiaries have been on increasingly sound financial footing, paying off the large bank loan at a rapid rate (see Balance Sheet).

To the best of our knowledge, no customer, competitor, supplier or shipper has ever been dissatisfied with the integrity of Roxco or its subsidiaries.

Comments — W. M. Towson, Director of Services of the parent company, is a first cousin by marriage of our Florida District Sales Manager, Jim Carr.

Recent Purchasing History

	\multicolumn{6}{c}{Purchases, $ Thousands}
	\multicolumn{2}{c}{TiO$_2$}	\multicolumn{2}{c}{Aliza tints}	\multicolumn{2}{c}{Other lines}
Branch and Location	1975	1974	1975	1974	1975	1974
Roxco, Ventura	143	120	33	32	14	14
Red Bluff	47	39	27	24	11	10
Red Lake	55	53	40	42	8	11
Everett	87	89	49	47	20	18
Jilprint, Warren	10	8	24	25	47	43
Danberry	49	43	57	63	82	73
Zip, Monterey	22	21	17	16	8	6
Chadd's Ford	12	11	9	8	5	5
Fremont	41	42	27	24	33	32
Edu-Paint, Half Moon Bay	1	1	3	2	—	—
Totals	467	427	286	283	228	212

APPENDIX B

An Industry Description

The following description of the thermosetting plastic resins industry was prepared by the Marketing Research Section of a chemical company (disguised by the fictional name, XYZCHEM Co.) that was contemplating the development and commercialization of a new resin, urea formthional. Although the report, prepared in 1960, is out of date as to many prices, production and consumption figures, it is a practical example of a typical industry description.

THE THERMOSETTING PLASTICS RESINS INDUSTRY
(with emphasis on molding markets)

In the following sections, the marketing of thermosetting resins is discussed. This information serves as a basis for further consideration of possible markets for urea formthional (UFS).

There are a large number of thermosetting materials used in the plastics industry. The predominent types of thermosets in sales volume are phenol formaldehyde, urea formaldehyde, and melamine formaldehyde. Many other materials — epoxies, alkyds, diallyl phthalate, etc. — are also thermosetting plastics. In order to simplify the end-use analysis of markets, the term, "thermoset", will refer only to the three major thermosetting resins in the rest of this report. Also the words, "melamine", "urea", and "phenolics" will be used here to mean the thermosetting resins of melamine formaldehyde, urea formaldehyde, and phenol formaldehyde.

Background

Two general classes of materials are produced by plastic resin manufacturers — thermosetting plastics and thermoplastics. Both types of materials are moldable into particular shapes by physical changes involving temperature and pressure. Unlike thermoplastics, thermosetting plastics also react chemically under the heat and pressure of molding. This difference reflects itself in the physical properties of the products obtained from these two types of materials.

The first plastic, cellulose nitrate, was a thermoplastic. It was first used in the 1870's for billiard balls and dentures. The material had many inherent limitations, but it led the way in product improvements and to other thermoplastics.

In the early 1900's, the second type of plastic materials, thermosets, was discovered. Phenol formaldehyde was the first thermosetting resin. Phenolics found such extensive use that by 1920, they were the largest selling plastic. Many current phenolics applications were among the earliest end uses of plastics. Examples of this are kitchen utensil handles, auto distributor caps, and buttons.

Phenolics are very versatile materials. For specific uses, a variety of modifications can be made to achieve particular property requirements. Over a period of time, hundreds of phenolic resins have been marketed. It is almost true that a phenolic resin is available for any known application, and phenolics were tried wherever a possible use could be found. Industry sources have stated that there are no new end uses for phenolics. This tends to illustrate the maturity of the phenolics markets.

In the late 20's and early 30's, cellulose acetate, a thermoplastic, challenged phenolics for sales supremacy among plastic materials. In the same years, the second major thermoset, urea formaldehyde, was introduced commercially. Ureas were slightly cheaper to manufacture than phenolics and overcame the major defect of phenolics, lack of colorability. However, ureas had defects of their own so that the advantages and disadvantages of urea formaldehyde relative to phenolics tended to balance out.

Ureas were molded in many of the phenolics applications. They captured molding markets only where the advantages in colorability were greatly needed. Decorative hardware, screw-type closures, and buttons were the main molded uses of urea formaldehydes. The largest market for urea resins has been in adhesives applications.

In the early 30's, du Pont supplied urea and formaldehyde to molding resin producers. American Cyanamid was the dominant domestic producer of urea resins because it had obtained in the early 30's several German patents on urea resins, including one on thiourea and formaldehyde compounds. Although not a manufacturer of urea resins, du Pont held a number of patents on materials and processes involving urea formaldehyes. A 1932 patent was granted to Du Pont covering urea formthional resins, but no companies showed interest in the material and the patent lapsed.

At the start of World War II, thermoplastics greatly surpassed thermosetting resins in volume usage. Styrenes and vinyls joined the acetates as leading thermoplastics. The polyolefins also came into being in the early 1940's to further emphasize the dominance of the thermoplastics in the plastics industry.

During the war, melamine formaldehyde thermosets were first commercially available. Melamines were more expensive materials, but they had some property advantages over the other thermosets. In World War II, melamines were molded into uniform buttons and dinnerware for our armed forces.

When military requirements fell off after the war, melamine molding resin sales virtually disappeared as the material found few uses where it could supplant the lower-priced phenolics and ureas. Since 1950, the melamine manufacturers have vigorously promoted their materials in two lucrative large-volume markets, dinnerware and decorative laminates. They have developed these markets with considerable success in recent years.

The essential point which appears from plastics history is that the thermosets are mature products. Both phenolics and ureas have been available in large volume for thirty years and seem to have passed through the period of greatest sales growth. Plastics molders are well acquainted with the favorable properties and also the limitations of thermosetting materials. Thermosets appear to have a well-defined niche in the plastics industry. Melamine resins could fill the thermosets niche as well as the other resins, but they are not competitively priced at present. Melamines do not now have widespread use, but they have certain superior properties which give them an advantage in specific markets.

Thermoset Resin Markets

The total consumption of thermosetting resins was 990 million pounds in 1959. Thus, the thermosets as a group may be classified with the other billion pound giants of the plastics industry — styrenes, vinyls, and polyolefins.

Of course, 1959 was the best sales year the thermoset resins have ever had. Thermoset sales have shown an upward trend throughout the 1950's with an inconsistent year-to-year growth pattern (see graph one). The total thermoset market has paralleled the economy as a whole in the last few years. Thermoset sales dipped in recession years and rose sharply during 1955 and 1959. This behavior contrasts to the explosive gains of the polyolefins during the same period.

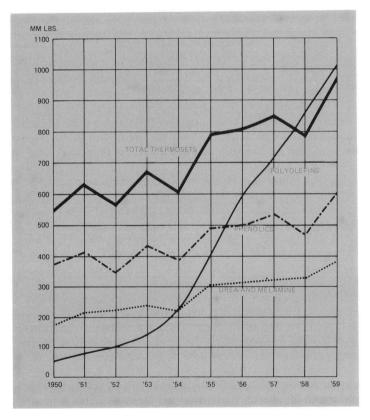

Graph One: Production of thermosetting and polyolefin plastics. 1950–1959*

*U.S. Tariff Commission Statistics. Because of captive thermoset plants, production rather than sales is shown.

Phenolics consumption has increased at an annual rate of 6% in the last ten years; urea and melamine, 12%. Also, fluctuations in sales of phenolics have been more severe than urea and melamine.

The major end-use markets for thermoset materials are bonding, coating, and molding. Bonding applications of thermosets are in plywood and laminating. A promising new bonding use has been for chipboard. Coating or treating uses are found in the textile and paper industries. Thermoset materials for protective and insulation purposes are also included in the coating category. Molded thermosets have applications in many markets. Table One indicates recent thermoset growth trends in these markets.

Table 1. Thermoset Market Growth, 1955–1959.

	Consumption, MM Lb.		% Sales Increase
	1955	1959	1955–1959
Bonding			
Phenolics	145	198	37
Urea & Melamine	122	159	30
	267	357	34
Coating (or Treating)			
Phenolics	77	115	49
Urea & Melamine	93	97	4
	170	212	25
Molding*			
Phenolics	200	218	9
Urea & Melamine	70	104	49
	270	322	19
Total			
Phenolics	489	604	24
Urea & Melamine	301	384	28
	790	988	25

*Includes approximately 50% filler by weight.

From 1955 to 1959, thermosets consumption in bonding markets has increased substantially. Phenolics growth has been greatest in coating markets. Urea and melamine have grown more in molding uses.

In summary, thermoset consumption has grown at a rate of roughly 8% per year in the past few years. This growth is at a slower rate than the plastics industry as a whole and has not been achieved in all of the thermoset markets.

Molding Resin Markets

Thermoset molding resin sales were 300 million pounds in 1959. Of this market, 200 million pounds were phenolics; 60 million pounds, melamine; and 40 million pounds, urea. Sales have been increasing at a rate of 9% per year in the last five years.

Graph two indicates the recent molding resin sales pattern for thermosets. While phenolics and ureas fluctuated in the same manner as the total thermoset market, melamine molding resin sales have shown a steady increase throughout the period.

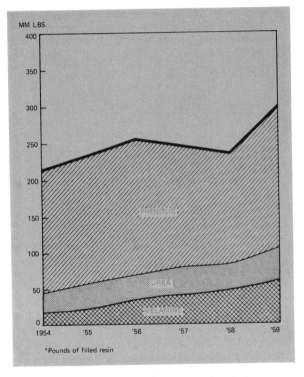

Graph Two. Thermoset molding resin sales*
1954—1959

The four largest end-use markets for thermosets are: (1) the electrical and electronic industry, (2) screw-cap closures, (3) appliance and kitchen utensil parts, and (4) dinnerware. These markets accounted for over four-fifths of thermoset molding resin sales in 1959. Phenolics and urea are used in the first two markets; phenolics, the third; and melamine, the fourth. (See graph three).

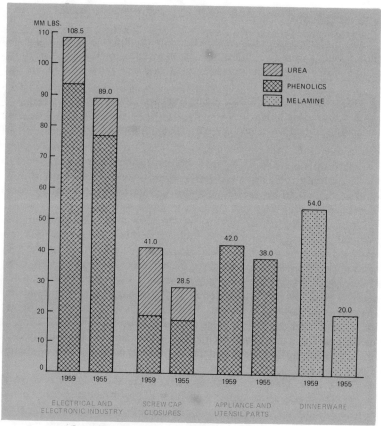

Graph Three. Thermoset end-use molding markets.
1955 and 1959

There are many uses for thermosetting materials in the electrical and electronics industries. For phenolics, the most important applications are for panel boards, switchgear housings, and familiar items like vacuum-tube bases and resistors. Phenolics are consumed in greater volume in the electrical part of this industry rather than in the more rapidly growing electronics segment of the business. Phenolics sales to these markets are often related to new construction of electrical facilities. Urea resins are molded into household wall plates for light switches and other wiring device parts. Phenolics account for nearly 90% of thermoset sales to the electrical and electronic industries.

Urea resins account for over half of thermoset consumption in screwtype closures. These are the tops for many bottles, cans, and squeeze tubes. Colorability of ureas is an important property in the consumer part of the closures market. Phenolics are used for liquor bottle tops and for commercial containers. Urea resin sales for the closures market have doubled in the last five years.

Phenolic resins have a firm place in appliance and kitchen utensil uses. Washing machine agitators and pot and pan handles account for most of this market. Hand appliance housings and decorative push-buttons also use phenolics and a small amount of urea resins. The rate of growth of thermoset sales in these uses is approximately the same as new household formation.

Although melamine is used in small volumes in the first three thermoset markets, its predominant molding application is for dinnerware.[1] Melamine sales in the dinnerware market increased over 150% from 1955 to 1959. This huge increase has been the result of several factors: (1) concerted and prolonged promotional efforts of resin manufacturers and dinnerware molders, (2) greatly improved styling and decorative patterns, and (3) acceptance by institutional users and young families because of durability. Melamine has made deep penetrations of the dinnerware market traditionally held by various ceramics. In contrast to other thermoset resin markets, melamine dinnerware appears to be in its greatest expansion phase.

There are many additional markets for thermosets besides the four just discussed. All three major thermosets are molded into buttons. Ureas took most of this market a few years ago, but a pearlescent polyester has become the industry standard recently. Melamines are specified for military uniforms buttons. Phenolics are used in such diverse applications as caster wheels, camera parts, and toilet seats. Phenolics also were the original materials for telephone bases and handsets, but colored thermoplastics have taken over this market. Electric razor housings were originally molded in phenolics, graduated to colored urea resins, and evolved to the use of melamine. These miscellaneous markets, which account for roughly one-fifth of thermosets consumption, have generally shown a declining use of thermosets over the past ten years.

In summary, these present thermoset markets are the first ones which a new thermoset molding resin, such as urea formthional, might be expected to penetrate. Most of these end-use markets consume large quantities of thermosetting materials. With the exception of the dinnerware market consumption of thermosets has not been increasing rapidly in molding applications.

Products and Prices

Thermosetting molding resins are available on the market in a wide variety and at a wider range of prices than is usually found with thermoplastics. There are many differences in the resins themselves, but the major factor in product variety is the use of filler materials in thermoset molding resins. Both the amount and type of filler markedly affect the price range and product line of available thermosets. Since moldings of unfilled thermoset polymers are very brittle, there are very few molded applications for unfilled thermosets. Each of the three major thermosets is available with many different fillers. The average amount of filler used in commercially available molding resins is usually estimated at 50%.

Filler materials range in price from less than a penny a pound for clays to sixty cents per pound for glass-impregnated fibers. Each filler imparts certain desirable properties in the final resins. Asbestos gives improved heat resistance; mica, better electrical properties; and so forth. Thus, the choice of a thermosetting resin for a

---

[1] See Table Six for a partial list of melamine dinnerware molders.

particular application involves a careful price-property compromise. In general, it can be expected that the resin chosen will have the maximum amount of the cheapest filler which will still give the required combination of physical properties. Table two indicates the effect of the filler variable on materials choice in thermoset applications.

Table two helps to answer a basic question about thermosets markets. If unfilled phenolics cost 39c/pound to manufacture and sell and unfilled ureas cost 28c/pound, why do phenolics sell in much greater volume than ureas? Phenolics have better general properties than ureas, but these can be diminished by using better fillers with the ureas. However, as can be seen in the table, ureas with a more costly filler, alpha-cellulose, have no property advantage over phenolics with a cheaper filler, wood-flour, at 50% filler by weight. Therefore, as has been seen in the actual market situation, ureas are used only where the one property advantage of colorability gives it an edge over phenolics.

The table indicates a 30-fold difference in impact strength of phenolic resins depending on the type of filler used. Similarly wide ranges of other physical properties are obtained with different fillers. Of course, a given filler improves some properties and degrades others. Thus the filler choice itself calls for a compromise.

The number of currently available phenolics reflects the effect of filler choice. There are roughly a hundred different phenolic resins on the market ranging in price from 19c/pound to $9/pound. In contrast, urea formaldehyde molding resins are available with two fillers. The alphacellulose filled urea sells for 32c/pound and the wood-flour filled variety sells at 18c/pound. This difference may indicate the inability of ureas to compete with phenolics on a combined price-property basis. Seven melamine resins are available ranging in price from 35c/pound to $1/pound.

It will be important to determine the effects of fillers on urea formthional. The new product may have the product breadth of phenolics or the limitations of ureas. In a final evaluation of opportunity, more information about the use of fillers with UFS should be known.

Competition

The competitive climate among thermoset resin producers is very complicated.[2] The number of producers, presence of captive plants, and apparent profitability of the thermosets business raise many questions.

There are several major competitors in the phenolics molding resin business. The three dominant producers are Durez Company (division of Hooker Chemical), Bakelite (division of Union Carbide), and General Electric. Other competitors include Borden Chemical, Plastics Engineering, Westinghouse, and a host of smaller firms. None of the larger firms in this group produces the other two thermosets. There are various complex organizations in phenolics production by these firms. Some of the companies are integrated back to captive sources of raw materials; others, like G. E. and Westinghouse, have captive molding facilities related to other products of the companies (i.e., electrical switchgear, appliances).

---

[2] See Table five for a list of U.S. suppliers.

Table 2. Thermoset Properties*

Resin	Tensile Strength (M psi)	Flexural Mod. (MM psi)	Izod Impact	CST (°F)**	HDT (°F)*** 264 psi	Flammability	Arc Resist. (Sec)
Phenolic (Woodflour Filled)	5–9	1.0–1.2	0.24–0.60	300–350	300–370	SE–1	Tracks
Phenolic (Asbestos Filled)	4.5–7.5	1.0–2.2	0.26–3.5	350–500	300–500	Nonburning	10–190
Phenolic (Glass Filled)	5–18	2.0–3.3	0.3–18.0	350–550	300–600	Nonburning	4–190
Melamine (Alpha Cellulose Filled)	7–13	1.3–1.6	0.24	210	350–370	SE–1	110–140
Melamine (Glass Filled)	5–10	2.4	0.35	300–400	400	SE–1	180
Urea (Alpha Cellulose Filled)	5.5–13	1.3–1.6	0.25–0.40	170	260–290	SE–1	80–150
Diallyl Phthalate (Glass Filled Short Fibers)	6.7–9.2	1.3	0.4–1.2	365–465	350–500	SE–1	125–180
Diallyl Phthalate ("Orlon" Fiber Filled)	6–6.8	0.7	0.55–8.0	250–350	320–400	SE–1	115–130
Alkyd-General Purpose (Glass Filled)	4–9.5	2.0	0.6–10.0	450	400–500	Slow to Nonburning	150–210
Polyester Premix (With Chopped Glass)	4–10	NA	1.5–16.0	300–350	>400	Burns/SE–1	120–240

*Definitions of these properties and the test methods used to measure them are given in the ASTM Handbook.
**Continuous service temperature.
***Heat distortion temperature.

127

In contrast to phenolics manufacturers, there are only two major producers of urea and melamine molding resins — American Cyanamid and Allied Chemical. A half dozen small firms also produce these thermosets, but they are not factors in the molding resin business. Anti-trust litigation now pending has alleged restraint of competition in this segment of the thermosets business. The suit mentions Cyanamid, Monsanto (also a producer of melamine raw material, but not the resin), Reichhold, and other firms.

An analysis of the probable return on investment also indicates that differences exist between the phenolics and melamine segments of the thermoset business.

Table 3. Return on Investment: Thermoset Molding Resins.

Resin	Filler	Cost of* Sales, c/Lb.	Market Price c/Lb.	Net* Return %
Phenolics	Wood Flour	15.1	18.7	8
Ureas	Alpha-cellulose	16.0	34.0	47
Melamines	Alpha-cellulose	24.0	47.0	45

*Cost of sales and total investments for return were calculated by XYZCHEM Marketing Research, Filler varieties are the major types in current use and market prices are as of 6/60.

The reasons for the differences in these businesses are undoubtedly very complex. Urea and melamine producers may not feel that lower prices will increase sales. Phenolics manufacturers may be willing to take a lower return on sales because much of the business is captive. There may also plainly be differences in competitive pressures. In any case, the competitive situation which would face a new thermoset must be carefully considered in the final decision to commercialize the product.

Comparison of Materials

The choice of materials for specific end uses is greatly influenced by the physical differences between materials. Table four gives a comparison of various low priced molding resins on the basis of a few physical properties. The purpose of this comparison is to establish the relative merits of the materials expected to compete with urea formthional.

Phenol formaldehyde is one of the lowest-priced resins available. Comparatively, urea and melamine are priced above several other materials shown in the table.This factor alone may explain thermoset market characteristics already discussed. Note that alpha-cellulose filled urea formthional at a projected price of 23c/pound would be close to high impact polystyrene on a cost per cubic inch basis.

Thermosets differ from thermoplastics in many ways. In general, thermosets are stiffer, heavier, more brittle, and processed at lower temperatures than thermoplastics. As shown in Table four, filled thermosets have a greater stiffness than thermoplastics. Thermosets also have better electrical and thermal resistance than

Table 4. Comparison of Molding Materials.

Thermoplastics THERMOSETS	A	B	C	D	E	F	G
Polystyrene, General Purpose	0.83	1.05–1.08	400–500	.25–.60	150–165	6–8	350–550
PHENOL FORMALDEHYDE. WOOD-FLOUR FILLED	0.99	1.32–1.55	800–1200	.24–.34	300–350	3.0–4.5	275–340
Polyethylene, Low Density	1.08	.912–.925	14–38	2–5	140–175	15–30	300–500
Polystyrene, High Impact	1.09	1.04–1.07	250–450	.7–3.0	120–170	4–10	375–600
Polyethylene, High Density	1.20	.942–.965	85–160	1–10	200	15–30	330–530
Polypropylene	1.37	.90–.91	100–160	.5–1.5	200–245	6	300–500
Polyvinyl Chloride	1.43	1.65–1.72	55–80	.3–1.0	160–200	19	220–350
UREA FORMALDEHYDE, ALPHA-CELLULOSE FILLED	1.85	1.48–1.52	1300–1400	.24–.28	170	2.2–3.6	275–350*
MELAMINE FORMALDEHYDE, ALPHA-CELLULOSE FILLED	2.55	1.47–1.52	1300	.24–.28	210	2.0–5.7	300–320

A—Cost, Cents/Cu. In., 6/60
B—Specific Gravity.
C—Modulus of Elastici, Tension, PSI X 10^3
D—Impact Strength, Notched, Izod, Ft.–Lbs./In., at Room Temp.
E—Heat Resistance, Maximum Recommended Continuous Svc. Temp. °F.
F—Thermal Coefficient of Expansion, Linear, Maximum per °C. X 10^{-5}
G—Transfer or Injection Molding Temperature, °F.

*Compression Molding Temperature.

Appendix B

Aerojet-General
Structural Plastics Div.
Azusa, Calif.
  phenolic

Allied Chemical Corp.
Plastics & Coal Chem. Div.
New York, N.Y.
  melamine, phenolic, urea

American Cyanamid Co.
Plastics & Resins Div.
New York, N.Y.
  melamine, urea

American Reinforced Plastics Co.
Los Angeles, Calif.
  phenolic

American Viscose Corp.
Philadelphia, Pa.
  urea

Calresin Co.
Div. of Kundsen Creamery Co.
Los Angeles, Calif.
  melamine, phenolic

Chemore Corp.
New York, N.Y.
  urea

Durez Plastics Div.
Hooker Chemical Co.
  phenolic

Fiberite Corp.
Winona, Minn.
  melamine, phenolic

Garfield Mfg. Co.
Wallington, N.J.
  melamine, phenolic

General Electric Co.
Chemical Materials Dept.
Pittsfield, Mass.
  phenolic

Raybestos-Manhattan, Inc.
Reinforced Plastics Dept.
Manheim, Pa.
  phenolic

Reichhold Chemicals, Inc.
White Plains, N.Y.
  phenolic

Rogers Corp.
Rogers, Conn.
  phenolic

Sylvan Plastics, Inc.
Philadelphia, Pa.
  urea

Synthetic Plastics
Newark, N.J.
  urea

Synvar Corp.
Wilmington, Del.
  phenolic

Gisholt Machine Co.
Madison, Wisc.
  melamine

Gordon Chemical, Inc.
Wilmington, Del.
  urea

Hastings Plastics, Inc.
Santa Monica, Calif.
  phenolic

Heresite & Chemical Co.
Manitowoc, Wisc.
  phenolic

Hewitt & Bros., Inc.
New York, N.Y.
  urea

Holman Mfg. Co., Inc.
Hoosick Falls, N.Y.
  melamine, phenolic urea

International Textile Co.
Chicago, Ill.
  melamine, phenolic

Lebec Chemical Corp.
Paramount, Calif.
  phenolic

Magnolia Plastics, Inc.
Chamblee, Ga.
  phenolic

Melamine Plastics, Inc.
Winona, Minn.
  melamine

Omni Products Corp.
New York, N.Y.
  phenolic

Plastics Engineering Co.
Sheboygan, Wisc.
  phenolic

U.S. Polymeric Chemicals, Inc.
Stamford, Conn.
  phenolic

Union Carbide Plastics Co.
Div. of Union Carbide Corp.
New York, N.Y.
  phenolic

Valite Div.
Valentine Sugars, Inc.
New Orleans, La.
  phenolic

Vacuum Chemical Corp.
Niagara Falls, N.Y.
  phenolic

Witte & Sons
Burlington, Iowa
  phenolic

*Does not include foreign manufacturers selling in this country.

130

Table 6. Melamine Dinnerware Molders*

American Plastics Corp. (Div. of Heyden-Newport) Chicago, Ill.	Lucent Corp. New York, N. Y.
Applied Plastics Div. (Keystone Brass) Erie, Pa.	Mallory Plastics, Inc. Chicago, Ill.
Boonton Molding Co. Boonton, N.J.	Nichols Plastic & Engineering Co. Los Angeles, Calif.
Branchell Co. St. Louis, Mo.	Northern Industrial Chemical Co. South Boston, Mass. (recently acquired Watertown Mfg. Co., Watertown, Conn., also a melamine dinnerware molder)
Bryant Div. (Westinghouse) Bridgeport, Conn.	Oneida Silversmiths Oneida, N.Y.
Chicago Molded Products Chicago, Ill.	Owens-Illinois Lake City, Pa.
Devine Food, Inc. Chicago, Ill.	Plastics Incorporated St. Paul, Minn.
Fostoria Glass Co. Moundsville, W. Va.	Plastics Manufacturing Co. Dallas, Texas
International Molded Plastics, Inc. Cleveland, Ohio	Plastic Masters New Buffalo, Mich.
Kenro Corp. Fredonia, Wisc.	Prolon Plastics (Div. Prophylactic Brush) Florence, Mass.
Lapcor Plastics Manitowoc, Wisc.	Royalon, Inc. Chicago, Ill.
Lenox Plastics, Inc. St. Louis, Mo.	Stetson China Co. Chicago, Ill.

*Partial list, probably 15 more firms in this business.

thermoplastics. One difference in properties strongly favors phenolics. This property is the higher service temperature which phenolics can withstand. There are many uses in which phenolics are preferred because of this property.

Properties are so greatly affected by filler choice that comparison of thermosets is very difficult; however, a few generalizations are possible. Strength and electrical resistance are increased as you go from phenolics to ureas to melamines. Phenolics have superior thermal properties, and melamines have slightly better resistance to solvents and sunlight. Ideally it would be preferable to consider specific uses and specific materials in order to determine the choice of a particular resin.

BIBLIOGRAPHY

A Basic Guide to Exporting, U.S. Dept. of Commerce, 1974 (?)

Amstutz, Arnold E., *Computer Simulation of Competitive Market Response*, The M.I.T. Press, 1967.

Armstrong, Howard I., "Marketing Research and the Growing Carpet Industry", Chemical Marketing Research Assn., Paper No. 635, Washington, D.C. Meeting, Feb. 12–14, 1969.

Borcherdt, Gerald T., "Design of the Marketing Program for a New Product", in Clewett (ed.), *Marketing's Role in Scientific Management*, Amer. Marketing Assn., 1957, pp. 58–73.

Buzzell, Robert D., Donald F. Cox and Rex V. Brown, *Marketing Research and Information Systems*, McGraw-Hill, 1969.

Chisholm, Roger K., and Gilbert R. Whitaker, Jr., *Forecasting Methods*, Irwin, 1971.

Clark, William A., and Donald E. Sexton, Jr., *Marketing and Management Science: A Synergism*, Irwin, 1970.

Commerce Today, (monthly), U.S. Dept. of Commerce.

Cox, Keith K., and Ben M. Enis, *The Marketing Research Process*, Goodyear, 1972.

Deschampsneufs, *Selling in Europe*, London Business Publications, 1963.

Dodge, H. Robert, *Industrial Marketing*, McGraw-Hill, 1970.

Drucker, Peter F., "New/Old Top Management Aids: The Executive Secretariat", *Harvard Business Review*, Sept.–Oct., 1975. pp. 6–8.

Farley, John U., "Information Systems, Buyer Behavior and Industrial Marketing Research", Chemical Marketing Research Assn., Paper No. 682, New York Meeting, Apr. 29–May 1, 1970.

Forrester, Jay W., *Industrial Dynamics*, The M.I.T. Press, 1961.

Gee, Robert E., "The Opportunity Criterion – A New Approach to the Evaluation of R. & D.", *Research Management*, May, 1972, pp. 64–71.

Giragosian, Newman H. (ed.), *Chemical Marketing Research*, Reinhold, 1967.

Giragosian, Newman H., "Econometric Models" Chemical Marketing Research Assn., Paper No. 999, Virginia Beach Meeting, Sept. 1976.

Green, Paul E., and Donald S. Tull, *Research for Marketing Decisions*, (2nd ed.), Prentice-Hall, 1970.

Hansen, Harry L., *Marketing: Text, Techniques and Cases*, Irwin, (4th ed.) 1977.

Hegeman, George B., *The Art of Price Forecasting*, A. D. Little, Inc., 1970 (?).

Heskett, James L., *Marketing*, Macmillan, 1976.

Hess, Sidney W., "Realigning Districts by Computer", *Wharton Quarterly*, Spring 1969, pp. 25–30.

Hirschman, Winifred B., "Profit from the Learning Curve", *Harvard Business Review*, Jan.–Feb., 1964, pp. 125–139.

Kidder, Russell C., private communication, Aug. 30, 1976.

King, William R., *Quantitative Analysis for Marketing Management*, McGraw-Hill, 1967.

Kotler, Philip, *Marketing Decision Making: A Model Building Approach*, Holt, Rinehart & Winston, 1971.

Kuehn, Alfred A., and Michael J. Hamburger, "A Heuristic Program for Locating Warehouses", *Management Science*, July, 1963, pp. 657–658.

Marketing, Business and Commercial Research in Industry, The Conference Board, 1964.

Marketing Information Guide, (monthly), U.S. Dept. of Commerce.

McCarthy, E. Jerome, *Basic Marketing* (5th ed.), Irwin, 1975.

Mitchell, Arnold *et al.*, *Handbook of Forecasting Techniques*, Stanford Research Institute, 1975.

Montgomery, David B., and Glen L. Urban, *Management Science in Marketing*, Prentice-Hall, 1969.

Bibliography

Nathanson, D. M., *Chemical Engineering Progress,* Nov., 1972, pp. 89–96.

Perspectives on Experience, The Boston Consulting Group, 1972.

Raiffa, H., and R. Schlaifer, *Applied Statistical Decision Theory,* Harvard Business School, 1961.

Richmond, Samuel, *Statistical Analysis,* Ronald, 1964.

Schoner, Bertram, and Kenneth P. Uhl, *Marketing Research: Information Systems and Decision Making,* (2nd ed.), Wiley, 1975.

Sexton, Donald E., Jr., "Estimating Marketing Policy Effects on Sales of a Frequently Purchased Product", *J. Marketing Research,* Vol. VII, Aug. 1970, pp. 338–347.

Simon, Leonard S., and Marshall Freimer, *Analytical Marketing,* Harcourt, Brace & World, 1970.

Stobaugh, Robert B., and Phillip L. Townsend, "Price Forecasting and Strategic Planning: The Case of Petrochemicals", *J. Marketing Research,* Vol. XII, No. 1, Feb. 1975, pp. 19–29.

Survey of Current Business (monthly), U.S. Dept. of Commerce.

Uyterhoeven, Hugo E. R., *et al., Strategy and Organization: Text and Cases in General Management,* Irwin, 1973.

Weber, John A., *Growth Opportunity Analysis,* Reston, 1976.

Whitfield, Ronald M., "Forecasting Techniques via Econometric Models", Chemical Marketing Research Assn., Paper No. 967, New York Meeting, May 1976.

Williams, Roger, Jr., *Technical Market Research,* Roger Williams Technical & Economic Services, Inc., 1962.

133

INDEX

135

136